Home Economics
Teacher Education

Significant Writings
In Home Economics
1911 - 1979

Home Economics
Teacher Education

Significant Writings In Home Economics: 1911 - 1979

Editor
Bonnie Rader
Department Chair of Home Economics
California State University
Long Beach

Yearbook 7/1987

Home Economics
Teacher Education Section
American Home Economics Association

Lithographed in U.S.A.

ISBN 0-02-676230-7

Yearbooks of the Teacher Education Section of the American Home Economics Association are produced and distributed by GLENCOE PUBLISHING COMPANY, Bennett & McKnight Division, 809 W. Detweiller Drive, Peoria, Illinois 61615

Orders and requests for information about cost and availability of yearbooks should be addressed to the company.

Yearbook Planning Committee

Sandra Miller (Chair)
Department of Vocational
  Education
University of Kentucky
Lexington, Kentucky 40506

Edna Page Anderson
College of Home Economics
South Dakota State University
Brookings, South Dakota 57007

Valerie Chamberlain
Home Economics Education
University of Vermont
Burlington, Vermont 05405

Donna Coomer (Editor)
Private Industry Council
Menomonie, Wisconsin 54751

Ruth Dohner (Past Editor)
Department of Vocational
  Education
The Ohio State University
Columbus, Ohio 43210

Helen Hall (Chair Elect)
Home Economics Education
University of Nevada—Reno
Reno, Nevada 89557

Francine Hultgren (Editor)
Home Economics Education
University of Maryland
College Park, Maryland 20742

Joanna Kister
Vocational Home Economics
Department of Education
Columbus, Ohio 43215

Janet Laster (Past Editor)
Department of Home Economics
The Ohio State University
Columbus, Ohio 43210

Mary Lou Liprie
Department of Individual and
  Family Studies
University of Delaware
Newark, Delaware 19711

Bonnie Rader (Editor)
Department of Home Economics
California State University
Long Beach, California 90840

Vila Rosenfeld
Department of Home
  Economics Education
East Carolina University
Greenville, North Carolina 27834

Helen Westlake
York Community High School
Elmhurst, Illinois 60126

Sue Smith
Home Economics Education
State Department of Education
Montgomery, Alabama 36130

Joan Wilkosz
Minneapolis Public Schools
Minneapolis, Minnesota 55413

Herma B. Williams (Editor)
Assistant to the President
  for Research
Bryn Mawr College
Bryn Mawr, Pennsylvania 19010

Beulah Wingett
Upper Arlington High School
Columbus, Ohio 43221

Author Biographies

At the time of the publication of the selected articles the authors were listed as follows:

Bane, Lita. 1928—President, American Home Economics Association. Her careers included positions in Home Economics Extension Service, Journalism, teaching, and administration.

Bell, Camille. 1979—Professor, Home Economics Education, Texas Tech. University.

Bevier, Isabel. 1917—Director of Household Science, University of Illinois.

Bivens, Gordon. 1975—Professor of Family Environment, Iowa State University.

Blackwell, Gordon. 1962—President, Florida State University.

Brown, Marjorie. 1967—Professor of Home Economics Education, University of Minnesota.

Carter, Enid. 1979—Home Economics teacher, Oneonta, New York.

Cross, Aleene. 1979—Professor of Home Economics Education, University of Georgia.

Dales, Ruth. 1959—Professor of Home and Family Life, Florida State University.

Hill, Alberta D. 1979—Dean, College of Home Economics, Washington State University, Pullman.

Hook, Nancy C. 1970—Doctoral student, Department of Family and Child Sciences at Michigan State University and an AHEA fellow.

Hoobler, Icie Macy. 1963—Consultant to the Merrill-Palmer Institute, Former member of the Food and Nutrition Board of the National Research Council and former President of the American Institute of Nutrition.

Horning, Leora. 1979—Professor, Home Economics Education, University of Nebraska.

Hurt, Mary Lee. 1959—Chairman of Home Economics Education, Michigan State University. 1969—Program officer in Home Economics Education. Division of Vocational and Technical Education of the Office of Education, United States Department of Health, Education and Welfare.

Justin, Margaret. 1929—President, American Home Economics Association.

Lehman, Ruth. 1960—Professor of Home Economics Education, School of Home Economics, Ohio State University.

McGrath, Earl J. 1968—Former United States Commissioner of Education-Director of Institute of Higher Education at Teachers College, Columbia University.

Paolucci, Beatrice. 1970—Professor of Family and Child Sciences, College of Home Economics, Michigan State University.

Richards, Ellen H. 1911—Honorary President, American Home Economics Association.

Scott, Dorothy. 1959—Head, Home Economics Education Division, Ohio State University.

Shears, Twyla. 1979—Professor, Home Economics Education, Pennsylvania State University.

Spafford, Ivol. 1948—Special Assignment for American Home Economics Association Criteria. Formerly Director of Curriculum Development, University of Minnesota. 1935-1940, and Alabama Department of Education, 1919-1934.

Weigley, Emma. 1976—Philadelphia, Pennsylvania.

Zuill, Frances. 1933—Head, Department of Home Economics, State University of Iowa.

FOREWORD

Beginning in 1981, the Home Economics Teacher Education Section of the American Home Economics Association has annually produced a yearbook. The first two volumes were somewhat historical in nature. Yearbook 1, *Sixty Significant Years*, addressed the development of the field of home economics education while Yearbook 2, *Seventy Significant Leaders*, focused on leaders who were recognized as having a hand in that development. The current Yearbook (Number 7), *Significant Writings in Home Economics 1911-1979*, is a companion piece to Yearbooks 1 and 2. It complements the content of the early yearbooks by concentrating on the history of the home economics movement and its impact on home economics teacher education.

The means of presenting Yearbook 7 content is through a compilation of specially selected articles from the *Journal of Home Economics*, an official organ of the American Home Economics Association. The articles are classics that are considered significant in shaping both home economics and home economics teacher education. Organized into time frames, they reflect the developmental status of the field and profession. In this context the field can be examined more systematically than otherwise might be possible. The possibilities for concentrated analysis, synthesis, and for stimulation of new thought in home economics is increased as the writings from well-known home economics leaders during different eras appear side by side. Seen in relationship one to another, they reveal the richness of thought during the evolutionary phases of the profession. At the same time, they provide insight and background information for charting the profession's future direction.

The Yearbook makes easier the task of those who wish to become acquainted with the foundations of the profession. It will be useful as a textbook, supplement to a textbook, or as a reference work.

No undertaking of this kind could succeed without the input of a number of individuals. Gratitude is expressed to editor Bonnie Rader, who assumed the leadership role for the Yearbook; the home economics teacher educators who helped identify the articles; the Yearbook Planning Committee members, who conceived the Yearbook theme and provided direction; the American Home Economics Association, which granted permission to reprint the *Journal* articles; and the article authors, many now deceased, for the rich legacy. Bennett & McKnight Publishing Company, a Division of Glencoe, Inc., is due special thanks for financing and distributing the yearbook series.

Sandra W. Miller, Chairperson
Home Economics Teacher Education Section
American Home Economics Association

PREFACE

Yearbook 7 provides a history of home economics through selected articles from the *Journal of Home Economics*. The writings span the years from 1911 to 1979, are written by well-known leaders in home economics, and are identified as benchmark articles by home economics teacher educators. Some have been used as teaching tools to clarify the philosophy and mission of home economics. Others have provided students as well as home economics professionals with a sense of pride and an awareness of home economics as a field of education and service.

Forty active or retired teacher educators were contacted and asked to identify ten or more publications or articles of less than book length, which they considered to be benchmarks for teacher education. Various materials which appeared on home economics education course reference lists or were considered "classics" by the teacher educators were submitted. Many documents were eliminated because they were too long for this project.

The criteria for selection of the articles were the following: (1) significance in shaping the field of home economics education, (2) appearance on bibliographies used in home economics education courses, (3) reflection of the philosophy of the total home economics movement as it related to teacher education, (4) length of the article, and (5) fit of the article into the progression of history as it unfolded and the four parts of the book took shape. The Home Economics Teacher Education Section Yearbook Planning Committee of the American Home Economics Association (AHEA) was involved in making some suggestions and lending its approval and support as the project came to fruition.

Articles from the *Journal* were selected to portray a chronology of events which affected home economics teacher education. The *Journal* has embraced the spirit of the home economics movement, while at the same time depicting the confusion and search for direction. It has served the profession well in documenting not only accomplishments but changes in philosophy. Yearbook 7 traces the history of the home economics profession for almost 70 years through the writings of leaders who contributed their thoughts and knowledge about the profession as it existed during a particular time.

This Yearbook is presented in four parts. Part I contains four articles and is entitled Development and Early Progress. The pioneer works of Ellen Richards, Isabel Bevier, Lita Bane, and Margaret Justin span the years from 1911 to 1929.

Part II, Refocusing on the Home and Family, encompasses the period from 1933 to 1959. The history of home economics during this time is captured by Frances Zuill, Ivol Spafford, Lita Bane, Mary Lee Hurt and Ruth Dales, and Dorothy Scott.

Part III of the Yearbook is entitled Impacts on New Directions. Articles published from 1960 to 1969 include authors Ruth Lehman, Gordon Blackwell, Icie Hoobler, Marjorie Brown, Earl McGrath, and Mary Lee Hurt and Margaret Alexander.

Part IV, Priorities for the 70's, covers the period from 1970 to 1979. It contains articles by Nancy Hook and Beatrice Paolucci; Mary Lee Hurt; and Gordon Bivens, Margaret Fitch, Gwendolyn Newkirk, Beatrice Paolucci, Em Riggs, Satenig St. Marie and Gladys Vaughn; and Alberta Hill, Twyla Shear, Camille Bell, Aleene Cross, Enid Carter, and Leora Horning.

Finally, Marjorie Brown's 1984 AHEA Commemorative Lecture is presented as an epilogue to this fascinating collection of articles.

This Yearbook was made possible by the efforts of contemporary Home Economics Education leaders. The assistance of the following individuals in identifying articles is gratefully acknowledged: Lena Bailey, Julia Dalrymple, Anna Gorman, Hazel Hatcher, Fern Horn, Amy Jean Knorr, Phyllis Lowe, Berenice Mallory, Doris Manning, Lela O'Toole, Dorothy Scott, Marguerite Scruggs, Eva Scully, Hazel Taylor Spitze, and Patricia Thompson. Appreciation is also expressed to Charlotte McCall, AHEA Home Economics Teacher Education Section Chairperson, 1981-83, for her help in requesting suggestions from teacher educators.

Bonnie Rader

TABLE OF CONTENTS

Part I
Development and Early Progress 1911-1929

Chapter

Part II
Refocusing on the Home and Family 1933-1959

Part III
Impacts on New Direction 1960-1969

Part IV
Priorities for the 70's 1970-1979

Epilogue

PART ONE

Development and Early Progress
1911 - 1929

Home Economics stands for the ideal home life for today unhampered by
traditions of the past, the utilization of all the resources of modern science
to improve home life, the freedom of the home from the dominance of
things and their due subordination to ideals, the simplicity in material
surroundings which will most free the spirit for the more important and
permanent interests of the home and of society.

Creed by Ellen H. Richards - 1898

"Home Economics in its most comprehensive sense is the study of the laws,
conditions, principles, and ideals which are concerned on the one hand
with man's immediate physical environment and on the other hand, with
his nature as a social being, and is the study especially of the relation between these two factors . . ."

Lake Placid Conference - 1902

The American home is the center of all American life. Home Economics
in the schools of today should endeavor to work towards the maintenance
of the best types of home and family life because they are vital forces in
the establishment of a sound democracy. Women and men together make
the homes of our land, and both should understand the problems of
homemaking and be able to work together to build the home of today
and of the future. Home Economics is a subject that centers around the
problems of the home and other institutions whose problems are of similar
nature.

TEACHING OF HOME ECONOMICS
Anna M. Cooley, et al - 1921

13

1

The Social Significance of the Home Economics Movement

Ellen H. Richards
Honorary President American Home Economics Association

No great change comes over the ideas and consequent actions of a community without some underlying, often undiscovered, cause. Frequently the cause remains a mystery for decades or centuries. Very often the observed result is attributed to the wrong chain of causes, so that any suggestion as to the motives impelling recent changes must be very modestly made.

But when one has been a part of a certain definite series of consecutive efforts, one may be pardoned for having an opinion as to the trend of the thought directing it. First, Home Economics means to the leaders economics in its original significance, household administration, domestic management. Political economists have usurped the word to mean *production* of wealth. In early times this was largely done within the domain of the household, but with the taking away of the producing interest through the rise of factory products, a gap was left in the carrying out of this theory, only now beginning to be filled by the new science, the economics of consumption. More than this, the civilization of the past has been developed, we believe, through the family home, the bond of mutual interest between parent and child, grandparent and grandchild, brother and sister, which makes cooperation under one roof possible. According to Herbert Spencer's view, "the convictions which create and maintain the monogamic family have become innate in our modern civilization."

The home has a distinct ethical as well as economic meaning. It should include mutual helpfulness in spiritual matters as well as mutual economic benefit. In America this economic function of the homestead as a producer of goods was taken away first by the cotton factory, then the wooden mills, the shoe factory, the western flour mills, etc. The growth of cities and the concentration of business took away even the production of the finished article from the raw material, of the garment from the cloth, of the edible food from the farm product. Restaurants and hotels throve apace, amusements were provided for both adults and children, until in many cities the family if they keep together at all merely sleep under one roof, perhaps with several other families, but have no common life and no common interests. Of course this is not a universal condition, but it is too common, and too increasingly so, for the student of social tendencies to contemplate with equanimity.

An early protest was made by Col. Carroll D. Wright, when he was Labor Commissioner of Massachusetts, and who sent Miss Clare de Graffenried in the early seventies to the Lowell factory mill-houses to get budgets. Mr. Edward Atkinson and Colonel Wright from the economic stand-point passed to the effect on society which a continuance of this extravagant and ill-managed household would have. When 70 percent of the mill wages went for food, a poorly balanced ration and badly cooked at that, too little was left for shelter and clothes. In the same decade certain thoughtful women in New York and Boston observed the ignorance of others than factory girls of the needs of a well managed household, and in the seventies both Miss Corson of New York and Miss Parloa of Boston opened cooking schools because the standard of the family table seemed to be deteriorating. And even before the study of sociology was talked of, careful observers of social conditions felt the ethical value of the meeting place, around the common board, of young and old, and of their *satisfaction* with what was provided.

This *satisfaction* means a certain favoring of individual tastes. "Mother's cake" means just the amount of flavor or consistency preferred by the child. The ethical value of the home table has doubtless always been recognized, but it is now more clearly seen to have its reasons deep in human nature. Food is the fundamental race factor. Satisfaction with it is essential to well-being. The loving thought given to its preparation, who knows how much it has to do with its value?

For many unformulated reasons, the philanthropist first, then the sociologist, has wakened to the idea of the family table as one of the strong factors in social righteousness, and hence the beginning of reforms naturally and instinctively took the form of classes for the teaching of cooking.

The seventies and eighties saw this as the main endeavor. Some sewing classes were formed in social settlements and among the shiftless, and a few society girls met in clubs either to cook or sew for fun, but *mothers* still knew how to use the needle. The economic pressure began to be more strongly felt after the business panics of about that time, it was found that too often the woman's hand had lost its cunning and her mind its grasp on everyday affairs. Relief work showed that among families discouragement, shiftlessness and disintegration threatened the foundations of society.

Sociology—socionomy as suggested by Michael Lane—as studies, began to take the place of mere philanthropy. "Arm chair philanthropy" as some have termed it, was not sufficient. Actual understanding of the causes of the deplorable conditions was demanded. For twenty-five years now, these studies have been making, now in one city, one university, now in another, by workers and students all over our land. For our purpose it will be sufficient to consider three phases of this general effort to stem the tide of degeneration. True, the pessimist does not try to stem it. But why is not Cologne Cathedral allowed to decay? Has it not outlived its usefulness? No, it is the expression of noble, inspiring thought worthy of the effort to preserve.

Why should a mere tendency, due to a spirit of greed or even to heedless speed, be accepted as an inevitable law? Why should the dearest traditions of the race be run down without protest? "When the nobler members of the race combine their efforts to protect the type won by their ancestors and supported by social science, a new set of causes enters the field and a new tendency offers its phenomena for observation. Minorities grow into majorities, and the mountain becomes a high road." Thus speaks Professor Charles R. Henderson. It sounds the note of hopefulness, of belief in moral force over the material factors, the power of mind over matter, the power of strong minds over weaker ones, the triumph of higher purpose over that lower purpose which finally makes a coward of its possessor.

The three factors to which we shall refer are the house as a home, the food, and the education required to grasp the facts of modern economic conditions and to cope with them.

It was natural that the food should be the first studied. When Mrs. Quincy A. Shaw, Louis Agassiz' daughter, felt compassion for the working man tempted to drink and considered what might be done for him, she maintained the New England Kitchen from 1890 to 1900, to devise some means of helping him to a good noonday meal, and of teaching his wife to prepare sustaining food. The story of the Kitchen is a fairy story. How its work became known; what failures nearly every other city saw in trying to copy it because of varying conditions not understood at first, because of deep race prejudice in favor of or against certain foods; how the state of Massachusetts made the Rumford Kitchen a part of its exhibit at the Chicago Exposition; how the adult man and his wife were found to be too slowly affected, and the effort was finally turned by the generosity of another woman, Mrs. Wm. V. Kellen, daughter of B.F. Sturtevant, to the lunches of school children, where it rests today, is a long tale. Food is a most important factor in race progress, but it is so fundamental that in a measure it takes care of itself. That is, man will not starve if any food is to be had, and so wonderfully adaptive is the human body that almost any food can be assimilated if need arises. Jane Addams in her book Twenty Years at Hull House tells of the woman who sounded the knell of the well meant reform coffee house in her remark, "I'd ruther eat what I'd ruther. I don't want to eat what's good for me."

Within six months of the beginning of the New England Kitchen and its studies of social conditions, it was found that while among the fairly well to do there was a great misuse of food, among the poor the social need was for decent and safe *shelter* rather than food. The latter was more familiar and more under their control.

From that time, greater and greater attention has been paid to housing questions. These are complicated by the gregarious tendencies of those who do not have the world's burdens on their shoulders as some of us think we have, or who have little resource outside of friendly talk.

A good example of the shelter difficulty is told by Weber in his paper on the growth of cities. A woman was found with half a dozen children in a cellar room in New York. The children were growing up pale and thin. The family was transported out into the country and given a cabin and piece of land to work on, and perhaps a goat or a cow. The philanthropist rubbed his hands with satisfaction—that family will take care of itself now. Within six months they were found back in the same old den. When berated for her return, the mother retorted, "Folks is more company nor stumps, anyhow."

Interest *in people* is the strongest tie. Isolation is the hardest to bear, hence the fear of being ostracised if one is different. It is this persistent trait, unconscious of it though she be, which affects the housewife when she buys what her neighbor already has. Fear of being different from others is the mainstay of fashion and its changes.

In Philadelphia in 1890, studies of St. Mary's Street quarter showed the pressing need of better shelter. In Chicago in 1892-97, at Hull House, the Fellowship of the Collegiate Alumni and the College Settlements Association made house to house studies of standards of living.

One important fact was brought out in all these cities. The day worker is too tired to go far out of the way to purchase food; not more than two or three blocks father away will a shop be patronized even if the food is better, and more often the flavor and combination liked by one nationality is abhorred by another. It would seem that public kitchens are not suited to American conditions.

The open kitchen planned to encourage *adult* patrons to ask how and why was also a failure, as had been most of the adult cooking classes.

About 1882 the first summer work was given to public school children in Boston. In 1884 the Teachers College took one of the sets of blocks showing the composition of the human body and income and outgo, which had been prepared in Boston, and began their career as leaders in this movement. Pratt Institute followed, and Drexel soon after. Mr. Edward Atkinson of Boston, the economist, and Dr. Thomas Egleston, the philanthropist metallurgical professor at Columbia, one and all began with the girl and boy: Manual training and domestic science. All this meant that children *were not* and apparently *could not* be taught the essential manipulations of keeping themselves clean and fed and clothed in their own homes. At least they could not learn the most effective ways. All these schools have been cautioned not to make the work *trade work*, and so they have sometimes given principles to the exclusion of sufficient practice.

Meanwhile the socalled homes have become more and more boarding houses—and young people have gone out into the world with less and less sense of responsibility until employers of young men and young women have rebelled. It is said that not only do the young people show themselves ignorant, but they do not wish to learn. All classes of society show the lack of any appreciation of work as *a duty* or of any return owed to society.

It became evident that something must be done, and the rise of schools of commerce and of agriculture for boys and of domestic science for girls is the outcome of the belief that in the early years each individual must be trained to take care of himself and not to need several others to wait upon him. Then he must know what responsibility for his own acts means.

This upheaval in educational ideals, the insistence upon the introduction of the manual and domestic arts into the curriculum, means nothing less than an effort to save our social fabric from what seems inevitable disintegration. It also emphasizes the belief of educators that the education gained in performing the various daily duties required of the members of a family group is of the highest moral value, a steadying spiritual force. Why has it been so universal that the woman's club retorted to those who urged study of home affairs: "We have enough of that; we wish to hear about Greece and Rome or the Philippines?" Does this not mean that these women were never taught to find anything but drudgery in their work?

Housekeeping has too often been drudgery, monotonous and wearisome, something to be endured. The merchant, the business man, and the manufacturer, as well as the engineer, have been *stimulated* by the new problems of our time. They have only worked the harder. The housewife has been told that she must stay in and do her work. This was preached at her, written at her, but no one of them all, save perhaps the Englishmen Lecky and H. G. Wells, saw the problem in its social significance, saw that the work of home making in this engineering age must be worked out on engineering principles, and with the cooperation of both trained men and women. The mechanical setting of life has become an important factor, and this new impulse which is showing itself so clearly today for the modified construction and operation of the family home is the final crown or seal of the conquest of the last stronghold of conservatism, the home keeper.

Tomorrow if not today, the woman who is to be really mistress of her house must be an engineer, so far as to be able to understand the use of machines, and to believe what she is told.

The emergence from the primitive condition was slow because the few of us who did show our heads were beaten down, and told we did not know. It required many college women (from some 50,000 college graduates) to build and run houses and families successfully, here one and there another, until the measure of meal has been leavened, and the bread has risen over the edge. Society *is* being reorganized, not in sudden explosive ways, but underneath all the froth and foam the yeast has been working. The world is going to the bad only if one believes that material progress is bad. If we can see the new heaven and the new earth in it then we may have faith in the future.

The human elements of love and sacrifice, of foresight and of faith, are going to persist and any apparent upheaval is only because of settling down into a more solid condition, a readjustment to circumstances like an earthquake.

The farsighted, who with ear to the ground have worked to secure a place in education for these subjects fundamental to the modern home, are now respectfully listened to.

It is universally conceded today—only a few wilfully blind or croaking pessimists excepted—that home keeping under modern conditions requires a knowledge of these conditions and a power of control of persons and machines only obtained through education or through bitter experience, and that education is the less costly.

When social conditions become adjusted to the new order, it will be seen how much gain in power the community has made, how much better worth while the people are. Have faith in the working out of the destiny of the race, be ready to accept the unaccustomed, to use the radium of social progress, to cure the ulcers of the old friction. What if a few mistakes are made? How else shall the truth be learned? Try all things and hold fast that which is good.

The Home Economics movement is an endeavor to hold the home and the welfare of children from slipping away over the cliff, by knowledge which will bring courage to combat the destructive tendencies. Is not a distinctive feature of our age one of overcoming the natural trend of things? If a river is by natural law wearing away its bank in a place we wish to keep, do we sit down and moan and say it is sad, but we cannot help it? No, that was the middle ages. We say, hold fast, and we cement the sides and confine or turn the river.

The ancient cities whose ruins are now being explored in Asia seem to have been abandoned because of failure of the water supply as the earth became dessicated, as for example our Zunis' home. Does such an event stop

19

us today? No, we bring water from hundreds of miles. Man has gained such control over nature, but then will he sit down before his own problems and say what are you going to do about it?

What if the *apparent* motion is toward cells to sleep in, and clubs to play bridge in, and amusements for evenings, and a strenuous business life run on piratical principles into which the women are drawn as decoy ducks? Because this seems to be the trend is there any reason to think it cannot be changed the moment a goodly portion of the thinking people stand face to face with the problem? I believe it *is* possible to solve the problem, but only if the aid of scientifically trained women is brought to work in harmony with the engineer who has accomplished so much.

Household engineering is the great need for material welfare, and social engineering for moral and ethical wellbeing. What else does this persistent forcing of scientific training to the front mean? If the state is to have good citizens, productive human beings, it must provide for the teaching of the essentials to those who are to become the parents of the next generation. No state can thrive while its citizens waste their resources of health, bodily energy, time, and brain power, any more than a nation may prosper that wastes its natural resources.

The teaching of domestic economy in the elementary school, and Home Economics in the higher, is intended to give the people a sense of *control* over their *environment* and to avert a panic as to the future.

The economics of consumption, including as it does the ethics of spending, must have a place in our higher education, preceded by manual dexterity and scientific information, which will lead to true economy in the use of time, energy, and money in the home life of the land. Education is obliged to take cognizance of the need, because the ideal American homestead, that place of busy industry, with occupation for the dozen children, no longer exists. Gone out of it are the industries, gone out of it are ten of the children, gone out of it in large measure is that sense of moral and religious responsibility which was the keystone of the whole.

The methods of work imposed by housing conditions are wasteful of time, energy, and money, and the people are restive, they know not why. As was said earlier, shelter was found by early students of social conditions to be most in need of remedy, so we see that, as C. R. Henderson has said:

> In the first place the state is beginning to offer positive aid to secure a suitable home for each family. A communistic habitation forces the members of a family to conform insensibly to communistic modes of thought. Paul Goehre, in his keen observations printed in Three Months in a German Workshop, interpreted this tendency in all clearness. The architecture of a city tenement house is to blame for the silent but certain transformation of the home into a sty. Instead of accepting this condition as inevitable,

like a law of nature, and accepting its consequences, all experience demands of those who believe in the monogamic family that they make a united and persistent fight on the evil which threatens the slowly acquired qualities secured in the highest form of the family. It would be unworthy of us to permit a great part of a modern population to descend again to the animal level from which the race has ascended only through aeons of struggle and difficulty. When we remember that very much, perhaps most of this progress has been dearly purchased at the cost of women by the appeal of her weakness and need and motherhood, we must all the more firmly resolve not to yield the field to a temporary effect of a needless result of neglect and avarice. As the evil conditions are merely the work of unwise and untaught communities, the cure will come from education of the same communities in wisdom and science and duty. What man has marred, man can make better.

It is not impossible to furnish a decent habitation for every productive laborer in all our great cities; many really humane people are overawed by the authority, the pompous and powerful assertions of "successful" men of affairs; and more often sleep while such men are forming secret conspiracies against national health and morality with the aid of legal talent hired to kill. Only when the social mind and conscience is educated and the entire community becomes intelligent and alert can legislation be secured which places all competitors on a level where humanity is possible.

Here again the monogamic family is the social interest at stake. It is a conflict for altars and fires. We are told that all these results are the effect of a natural uniform tendency in the progress of the business world, and that it is useless to combat it. Professor Henderson reminds us that the tendency to uniformity revealed by statistics may be reversed when resolute men and women, possessed of higher ideals, unite to resist it. Jacob A. Riis holds that these evils are not by a decree of fate but are the result of positive wrong, and in his dedication of his account Ten Years' War we read "to the fainthearted and those of little faith this volume is reproachfully inscribed by the author."

In like manner we call today for more faith in a way out of the slough of despond, more resolute endeavor to improve social and economic conditions, and we beg the leaders of public opinion to pause before they condemn the efforts making to teach those means of social control which may build yet again a home life which will prove the nursery of good citizens and of efficient men and women with a sense of responsibility to God and man for the use they make of their lives.

2

The Development of Home Economics

Isabel Bevier
Director of Household Science, University of Illinois

In the JOURNAL for October, 1911, a memorial number for Mrs. Ellen H. Richards, there is a review of the development of Home Economics in the United States. It is the purpose of this article to give some idea of the progress of the subject in the United States since that time.

As will be seen by reference to the article mentioned, by 1911 Home Economics was at least on trial in quite a variety of organizations and institutions. It was included in the curriculum of many public and private schools, practically all of the state universities and Land Grant colleges, and in many endowed institutions. Women's clubs, Young Women's Christian Associations, and many philanthropic organizations had sought its aid in their work.

Owing to the fact that the agricultural colleges had put emphasis upon the scientific phases of the work, the term "scientific" was perhaps a little over-worked at that time, and led the housekeeper to announce that she did not know anything about science, but she *could* cook.

A study of the JOURNAL for the past five years gives one the impression that this period has been one of steady growth and adaptation of Home Economics to a great many types of work and also that there has been an attempt at standardization, not only of the subject matter to be taught, but also of the methods of teaching it. For example, a differentiation of high school from college work was easily made on the use of the word, "scientific." It was evident that while it was possible in college courses to have a strong basis of science, such a plan was quite impossible in the high school, in so far as the content of the course was concerned. There the term, "scientific," referred to the method to be used. The part upon which emphasis could be placed for the student was careful manipulation, cost, and the digestion of food connected with the student's knowledge of physiology. The reaction from the overworking of the term, "scientific", led to undue emphasis upon the word, "practical", as though the two terms must of necessity be opposing ones, and great stress was placed upon the so-called "practical courses" with emphasis upon skill in manipulation, the cost and quality of the finished product, and this "practice" idea was aided by the establishment later of the practice houses or apartments as a feature of the work.

The criticism of these houses is: first, that the standard of living is too costly, both as regards time and money expended; second, that so many students do the work that no one individual is responsible for any part of the result; third, that conditions are so abnormal that the practice housekeeping has little value. Notwithstanding the criticism, the first experimental house, which was at the University of Illinois, 1908, has been followed by many others, notably, Rock Hill, South Carolina; Denton, Texas; Pratt Institute; Wisconsin; Cornell; and Mississippi State College for Women; and some form of practice housekeeping is offered now in most institutions.

The same idea emphasized household management courses as part of the preparation of the manager of an institution. All these are but indications of the public appreciation of the breadth of the subject and the recognition of its ability to help in the solution of the problems of daily life. Gradually the public conception grew to the realization that Home Economics meant not only selection and preparation of food, but that its goal was really the improvement of the home. Accordingly, one finds in the literature pleas for courses on the home, notices of special courses offered for homemakers, and suggestions for the study of the family and for art in the home.

Home Economics did not escape that watchword, "efficiency," and the promoters of scientific management found a wide field for effort in the haphazard business of housekeeping. This realization that Home Economics was working for the home, and seeking to enable the woman to see the home in its larger aspects and her part and place in it, led very naturally to emphasis on the economic questions involved in home management and furnishing, and the words "division of income" and "family budgets" were added to the vocabulary of Home Economics. Any serious study of the home, its processes and products, disclosed at once the fact that many questions concerning time-honored practices could not be answered, and pointed very clearly to the need for research, and so that phase of the subject received attention. Home Economics had profited greatly by the research in the problems of nutrition, but it began to be realized that many of the questions concerning household processes were most likely to be solved by women; witness the answer to the question, "What makes jelly jell?"

While the homemaker was especially interested in the food problem within the home, the social worker, the teacher, and the physician were working at the problem of food for the child in school, and thus a new impetus was given to the study of that very important question, the feeding of school children. School boards took up this question and provision was made in many school buildings for the serving of lunches under the direction of the teacher of Home Economics and as a part of her regular duties.

Once this connection between food and health was recognized, many new lines of work were suggested, such as the housing problem, and the clothing question. Indeed, a new profession was opened to women, viz., that of the dietitian. Ordinary people began to understand that the term, "diet," was not confined to the sick room. This change in public sentiment led to courses for the training of people who should understand how to feed both the well and the sick, the child and the adult, and courses for the training of dietitians, as well as for lunchroom manager, were added to the curriculum, and the terms, "standard diet" and "basal ration" came into general use.

It was in the year 1912 that the American Home Economics Association gave proof of the development of the subject within its own ranks by the publication of *The Syllabus of Home Economics*. This syllabus represented the work of a committee for more than two years. Its purpose as stated in the syllabus is "to classify in logical order the various topics which can properly be included under the term, 'Home Economics.' " One proof of growth in the conception of the subject is shown by the fact that a fourth division, household and institution management, was added to the three original ones, food, clothing, and shelter, showing the gain in appreciation of the social significance of the work. In connection with this idea of the social value of the work, one can offer as proof the specific work of the government for one class of people. While not officially connected with Home Economics, it is so closely allied with it as to warrant consideration.

Reference is made to the questionnaire on Home and Woman sent out October, 1913, by Secretary Houston of the Department of Agriculture. The point of view of the Secretary is given in the following quotations:

THE WOMAN ON THE FARM

The woman on the farm is a most important economic factor in agriculture. Her domestic work undoubtedly has a direct bearing on the efficiency of the field workers, her handling of the home and its surroundings contributes to the cash intake, and, in addition, hers is largely the responsibility for contributing the social and other features which make farm life satisfactory and pleasurable. On her rests largely the moral and mental development of the children, and on her attitude depends in great part the important question of whether the succeeding generation will continue to farm or will seek the allurements of life in the cities.

24

The department believes that intelligent help to women in matters of home management will contribute directly to the agricultural success of the farm. It purposes, therefore, to ask Congress for means and authority to make more complete studies of domestic conditions on the farm, to experiment with labor-saving devices and methods, and to study completely the question of practical sanitation and hygienic protection for the farm family.

The farmer's wife rarely has access to the cities where labor-saving devices are on competitive exhibit, nor does she often meet with other women who are trying these devices and gain from them first hand information. It seems important, therefore, that the department, cooperating with the proper state institutions, should be ready to give the farm home practical advice. Some work has already been accomplished in studying the problems of nutrition and advising the women in the country as to the economical use of various foods and methods of using these foods to obtain variety in diet. Apparently there is need also for advice on general diets that will be healthful and varied, because the farm home usually has but a limited number of foods at its disposal and has not the opportunity to add novelties to the diet, such as the city woman finds in her convenient store.

Such a serious attempt on the part of the government to find out actual living conditions among farm women was most encouraging proof of the fact that Home Economics was making for itself a large place in the thoughts of the people.

It was in this year, too, that the United States Government, through another great department, made a contribution to the work of Home Economics by its recognition of the claims of mother and child in the work of the Children's Bureau.

The year 1914 affords substantial proof of the possibility and desirability of combining some phases of Home Economics with many forms of social work. Types of these combinations are visiting housekeepers, work with settlements, such as the connection made between Simmons College and the settlements of Boston, the housekeeping centers of many cities, and the food work done in connection with the social welfare work of many manufacturing plants. Mention must be made, also, of the excellent work in Home Economics by the National Federation of Women's Clubs under the skillful guidance of Miss Helen Louise Johnson.

It was in this year, too, that additional proof of interest in and appreciation of the value of Home Economics was shown by another great branch of the government, the United States Bureau of Education, by the publication of a series of bulletins on Education for the Home. The reasons for such a publication are given in part by the following quotation:

For most people the home is the beginning and end of life. All their activities proceed from it and return to it. Therefore, of all the arts those pertaining to homemaking are the most important and of all the sciences those which find their application in the home, making us intelligent about the home and its needs, are the most significant.

If the schools are to assist in making us intelligent about the life we live and the work we do, they must provide liberally for instruction in these arts and sciences. Within the last two or three decades, educators and people generally have become conscious of this fact as never before, and gradually the schools are being readjusted to meet the new demands. Probably they have never undertaken a more important or difficult task, and there is constant need for information in regard to methods adopted and results obtained.

Home Economics has official recognition for the first time in this year by taking its place beside Agriculture in the published list of the workers in "Agriculture and Home Economics" in the Department of Agriculture. The word, "extension," is written large in the records of this year, which find an appropriate climax in the passage of the Smith-Lever Act in May, 1914.

The year 1915 stands quite alone as a banner year for Home Economics because of the important legislation of the United States government concerning it. While the Smith-Lever Bill was signed by the President in May, 1914, the plans for its administration were not completed until 1915. This bill is distinguished, not only by the fact that it is the first specific legislation for the home by the Federal Government, but also by the magnitude of the resources it makes available. No single legislative act has brought to Home Economics either so great opportunities or such serious obligations.

The Smith-Lever Act makes provision for "cooperative agricultural extension work which shall consist of the giving of instruction and practical demonstrations in Agriculture and Home Economics to persons not attending nor resident in the agricultural college." In the plans for the administration of this bill, the States Relations Service was organized under the leadership of that friend of Home Economics, Dr. A. C. True, who has for so many years aided in the development of the subject through the publications of the Office of Experiment Stations, and as a member of the committee on nomenclature of the American Home Economics Association. The scope of the work previously included in nutrition investigations was extended to include studies of clothing, household equipment, and household labor, thus constituting the Office of Home Economics under the able guidance of Dr. C. F. Langworthy, for a long time identified with work in Home Economics.

This year was further signalized by another very important event in another department of the United States government, viz., the Bureau of Education, by the appointment of two specialists in Home Economics, Mrs. Henrietta Calvin and Miss Carrie M. Lyford.

There is yet a third feature of legislation, which, while it has not materialized, is significant of the trend of the times. This idea found expression in the Smith-Hughes Bill of the last two Congresses. "This bill would provide Federal aid to cooperate with the various states in the maintenance and support of vocational schools of Agriculture and Home Economics and the trades and industries for persons fourteen years of age and over, and in the maintenance and support of schools for training teachers for the vocational subjects in these vocational schools." The vocational school seems at present the phase most in the public eye. What can Home Economics do for it? What will it do for Home Economics? Both questions are as yet unanswered. To some it seems certain that the vocational school will revise very greatly the methods of teaching Home Economics. To others there seems some danger that Home Economics in the vocational school shall be judged solely by its power to produce commercial products.

Yet another bill is indicative of the thoughts of some of the people and their desire to promote research in Home Economics. This is known as the Smoot Bill, which would provide Federal aid for research or experimentation in Home Economics at the Experiment Stations of the Land Grant Colleges.

If the JOURNAL may be taken as an index of the spirit and achievements of the work of Home Economics, it would appear that the art side has not been in the public mind as much as the other phases of the work. That condition might be explained on the old theory that the necessities of life, such as food, clothing, and shelter, must be met first, but surely the newer conception of life recognizes that beauty is an essential factor of all right living, and imposes upon every individual the responsibility to make some contribution to the beauty of life.

Thus it appears that in the past five years Home Economics has done much intensive work in classifying and arranging its material, in separating essentials from non-essentials, in improving the methods of presentation, and in interpreting the aim and scope of its work. It has been interested in the home, the school, and that larger field outside the home. It has done much to improve child life, both through its own agencies and in connection with other agencies. It has been found useful by the social worker, the teacher, the philanthropist, and the statesman. It has influenced the private home, the public press, and legislation. It has lived up to its motto, "For those interested in Homemaking, Institution Management, and Educational Work in Home Economics." May it go forward and deeper with a brave heart.

3

Home Economics
Outward Bound

Lita Bane
President, American Home Economics Association

In December of this year the American Home Economics Association will have been organized twenty years. It seems fitting, therefore, that we review briefly our two decades of history. The facts will doubtless be given in more detail at our next annual meeting when we hope to celebrate the twentieth anniversary of our incorporation, which took place in 1909.

The soil for the organization had been carefully cultivated through the Lake Placid Conferences, 1899 to 1908, and due largely to this fact the organization has thrived since its beginning.

In 1908 we had a general membership of 830 with no affiliated state organizations, no affiliated student clubs, no magazine, and no regularly employed personnel. Today we have a total membership of 9251, affiliated state organizations in 47 of the 48 states, one in the District of Columbia, two affiliated groups in Canada, one in Edmonton and another in Nova Scotia, one in Porto Rico and another in Hawaii. We have single memberships in Australia, Scotland, Esthonia, and Turkey. We have 571 affiliated student clubs. We have a monthly magazine and a quarterly bulletin with a full-time editor, a part-time abstractor, and a business manager. We have a full time executive secretary and a special field worker in the field of child development and parental education. In 1920 our gross income was $14,841; in 1928, $54,029. In 1920 the treasurer handled $24,071; in 1928, $111,033.

Our Association has undoubtedly been influential in promoting the teaching of home economics. Reports show that 627 of our 1,150 institutions of higher learning (more than half) have home economics departments. Two hundred and sixty-five cities, 48 states, and two territories have home economics supervisors. There are some fourteen hundred persons engaged in home

28

economics extension work. If we should add to these the large number of home economics teachers in elementary and secondary schools, we should have an impressive number.

It would be impossible to mention all of the women and men who have been responsible for this forward march of home economics but I pause to pay tribute to some of our pioneers: Mrs. Ellen H. Richards, Caroline L. Hunt, Mrs. Alice Peloubet Norton, Mr. and Mrs. Melville Dewey, W. O. Atwater, C. F. Langworthy, Anna Barrows, A. C. True, B. R. Andrews, Isabel Bevier, and Abby Marlatt—all names appearing again and again in the early records of our organization.

We are gratified with the progress our organization has made, with the advance which home economics has made. Perhaps we might profit, however, by looking back just a little to see what our commission actually was and by inquiring whether we have proceeded along the path that was charted by these courageous, large-minded, far-seeing pioneers. We find the first Lake Placid Conference asked these questions which I believe are well worth asking ourselves frequently:

What are the essentials that must be retained in a house that is a home?

What may be better done outside, what standards must be maintained inside?

What must be acquired by practice and what may be learned from books?

What must go into the curriculum for the lower schools and what is the duty of the higher education and the professional school?

Finally, what forces in the community can be roused to action to secure for the coming race the benefits of the twentieth century progress?

In the report of the same conference we find the following: "After full discussion, the name 'Home Economics' was agreed on as the title preferable for the whole general subject and it was determined to consider it a distinct section of the general subject of economics."

And in 1902 as follows:

A study of sociology is necessary to the right understanding of the relation of the home to the whole social structure. The homemaker needs to know the purpose of the home, the degree of importance in relation to other things in life.

Home Economics in its most comprehensive sense is that the study of the laws, conditions, principles, and ideals which are concerned on the one hand with man's immediate physical environment and on the other hand with his nature as a social being, and is the study specially of the relation between these two factors.

In a narrow sense the term is given to the study of the empirical sciences with special reference to the practical problems of house work, cooking, etc.

In forming a complete definition, however, it may be possible to consider home economics as a philosophical subject, i.e., a study of relation, while the subjects on which it depends, i.e., economics, sociology, chemistry, hygiene, and others are empirical in their nature and concerned with events and phenomena.

. . . Almost every school or college above grade of high schools pretends to have departments of economics and philosophy as well as natural science. What is possible in such schools even is something to bind together into a consistent whole the pieces of knowledge at present unrelated.

There appears also this interesting comment by Marian Talbot:

It is sometimes thought that the differentiation (through elective courses) of women's education from men's in the two latter years of college will make it possible to introduce special courses in home economics. This opinion in the last analysis seems to imply that courses should be offered in special housekeeping activities of women, like cooking, sewing, and laundry work and that there should be parallel courses for college boys in putting down carpets, taking care of the furnace, and sweeping the sidewalk.

Again in 1903 we find the following statement:

History, sociology, and economics deal with fundamental problems of the family and the home. Biology, chemistry, and physics have important application in the household.

The following statements made by Mrs. Richards at the same meeting have suggestions in them for us today, twenty-five years later:

Only a superficial and erroneous idea can be gained from the study of social economics if a training in the older and well thought out science of economics, history, and logic is wanting.

But after all is said, the *great* field in home economics is in the line of original research and belongs in a graduate course and in such universities as are well equipped for it. Manual training schools and domestic science courses in small colleges are often offering work along lines not yet explored. The student is thus cheated into supposing he has a knowledge which the world does not possess.

The criticism has sometimes been made and justly, I believe, that the administration and direction of the American Home Economics Association has been too much in the hands of college people. The following statement made by Mrs. Richards and appearing in the 1906 Lake Placid report may help to explain why college people have been particulary active:

Our committee on higher education has had to bear the brunt of the battles, for when this conference came into existence eight years ago the fight was practically won in the elementary schools. It was only a question of ways and means, the leaver had begun to work. The hypodermic needle has given a little inflamation here and there, but academic opinion is yet impervious to the idea that the ethics of food and dress and household expenditure are the real moral philosophy problems of today and that no person can be considered educated who is ignorant of man himself and means at his hand for making a man.

In 1907, twenty-one years ago, we find the following:

Miss Day of the University of Missouri is advocating a nursery course for teaching the care of children from birth to kindergarten. Students have a chance to learn how to raise pigs and cows, why not teach them how to care for children? This project was at first laughed at but treated more seriously when better understood.

In 1908, we find the following statement appearing in the Lake Placid Quarterly Bulletin:

The American Home Economics Association will seek to bring together teachers of home economics and related subjects, superintendents and masters of schools, parents, physicians, health officers, architects, tenement-house inspectors, settlement workers, and students of social and civic affairs. Each of these groups has some valuable contributions to make and some suggestions to offer with reference to the means by which formal and informal educational enterprises relating to the home shall be promoted.

This brief review of the ideals of our pioneers would seem to indicate that we have yet to realize the full contributions which economics and sociology have to offer to our field of study and perhaps also we have not cooperated to the fullest with related groups and individuals. There are indications that on both of these points the immediate future will show considerable progress.

We have behind us twenty years of fine accomplishment, twenty years of growth, of adaptation to new demands, twenty years of developing ideas in this new field. Because our organization has come quickly into its present size and scope we must needs consider from time to time the best methods for its membership.

At present we are much like some houses which show plainly that additions and lean-to's have been built without any very logical plan, the chief aim being to take care of an ever increasing family. The time has come, however, when we can well consider the advisability of building a new structure to house our family, considering what rooms we shall need to care for the interests of the various groups, which rooms should communicate easily with one another, how large these rooms shall be, best methods for securing harmony, balance and unity in the entire organization structure. At this meeting a committee will report its recommendation for accomplishing this result. Perhaps the largest group not having any particular room assigned to them is the group of city supervisors and teachers. They have formed an informal organization which met yesterday and which will doubtless be incorporated in our revised organization plan.

Many persons in this group have been active workers in the association for years. One of the chief activities of this group will doubtless be the promotion of better home economics supervision and the placing of supervisors in more cities in order that home economics teaching may be done more effectively.

The field of our subject matter, though well set forth in our syllabus published in 1913, needs to be redefined in the light of present day interpretations of home economics and the advance of scientific discovery. On this point also a committee will make recommendations at this meeting.

Like all money spending organizations, we need a carefully made financial plan which will look forward to future spending and guide our expenditures into channels which will bring the greatest good to our profession. Such a committee has been at work during the past year and has its plan ready for presentation at this meeting.

Since home economists are trained to meet problems of feeding and care of families, I believe we should stand ready to assist when floods and other national disasters, such as we have found during the past few years, occur. I believe our program of work should provide some plan by which we can cooperate effectively in such emergencies. The American Red Cross reports helpful participation during the past few years, and we can doubtless offer still fuller cooperation in the future.

While our association is dealing with a great many significant problems, there are others of which we are conscious, although in some cases they have not been clearly formulated.

Everywhere our courses of study need to be carefully examined to see that we are not duplicating material. Surely after twenty years of experience we should be able to agree in a general way upon subject matter and methods suited to elementary, to secondary, to college work. Not only this, but we need to make sure that we are not duplicating work being better done in other branches of study. It sometimes happens that because of training and equipment another department can well do what we once did and we can move on to some new field, the needs of the home being sufficiently large to present unsolved problems for years to come. There is an increasing tendency in many fields to make practical applications of subject matter taught. I believe home economics with its emphasis on making practical use of scientific information can claim some credit for bringing about this situation, and that we can profit by it. It need not result in duplication but in releasing time for the student to broaden her interests or to develop in more detail some special interest.

In some instances, we have added course upon course without pausing to examine critically the content and significance of each. It is my belief that many courses once necessary in college can now be carried by high schools thus relieving the already too heavily loaded schedule of the college student, that in some cases two or even three dilute courses could well be combined to make one stimulating, meaningful course. We need to have the courage to be extremely critical, to learn to say "good-bye" to outgrown methods and subject matter, to insist upon high standards and scholarly attainment, and to be generous in sharing with other departments vital subject matter which might well fall in their field.

I regret any tendencies to mortgage more heavily the student's time for purely technical or vocational subjects and I would include in this, courses in the technique of teaching. In most cases I have known, this large emphasis on techniques has been a source of regret to the student after she has been out of college for a few years though the notes in her note-book may seem to be her salvation for her first few years out of school. Common sense tells us that the undergraduate curriculum cannot train adequately in general culture and insure at the same time expertness in any considerable number of techniques. At this point I believe we shall have to take a slightly altered point of view from that held in some quarters at the present time. Rather than attempting to perfect techniques in our laboratories, we can in many instances have appreciation and discrimination as our goal; and as an art course offers experience in designing and an English course may require students to write a sonnet, so we may offer practice knowing that as only a few students will ever make designing or writing sonnets their life work, so many of our students may not in the future make any great use of their training in the construction of garments or even the cooking of food. And if proficiency in techniques is needed, practice will have to be afforded through extra curricular activities, summer sessions, training in technical schools, or the serving of apprenticeships. Some of us would agree that techniques are more easily acquired outside college walls than are attitudes, ideals, appreciation, and certain habits of discriminating thought and that our greatest need is for bread, sturdy foundations, touch with many fields, that we may be adaptable and resourceful and equipped to fully enjoy what life offers and to direct others that they may enjoy it too. It is quite as true today as it was forty-five years ago when Olive Schreiner wrote of motherhood.

It is the work that demands the broadest culture. . . . . The lawyer may see no deeper than his law-books, and the chemist see no further than the windows of his laboratory, and they may do their work well. But the woman who does woman's work needs a many-sided, multiform culture, the heights and depths of human life must not be beyond the reach of her vision, she must have knowledge of men and things in many states, a wide catholicity of sympathy, the strength that springs from knowledge, and the magnanimity which springs from strength. We bear the world, and we make it. The souls of little children are marvellously delicate and tender things and keep forever the shadow that first falls on them, and that is the mother's.

I believe we need more of what Dr. Snedden has called "cultural home economics." I agree with his statement that it should produce a "vision, taste, perspective and aspirations far broader than can be reached by any vocational course."

Perhaps we could accomplish this in part by indicating to home economics students when they enter the home economics course something of the total problem of homemaking and pointing out to them the fields of study in the arts and sciences that contribute to the solution of these problems. Perhaps then, they would approach the fields of study with more interest and insight and would come away from them with more and better material bearing on home problems. And at the end of a course could we, in gathering together our results, point out their relation to other fields of study, thus giving a sense of relationship and unity? Not only must we keep abreast of rapidly changing fields of subject matter but we find ourselves called upon to interpret the needs of a rapidly changing home, a home in an entirely new setting, a money dominated economy, a machine run, and highly specialized age.

It seems likely that with our present efficient forms of production the home cannot for long, if indeed it can at the present time, compete with industry in a way that will be of any economic advantage to the home. Most things can be produced most efficiently on a large scale and by standardized methods.

What then is the function of the homemaker in the present economic order? Should she try to turn her home into a miniature factory with herself as chief managing engineer as well as being the workman, the clerical staff, and all the rest, with mechanical efficiency as her standard?

Or perhaps we believe in specialization and socialization of household tasks and agree with Heywood Broun, when he says,

Cooking is not an instinct. It's a gift.

There have never been enough good cooks to go around. Faced with a shortage, the state should step in and deny to all experts the privilege of functioning for a few instead of for the many. Let us suppose that somewhere

34

south of the Harlem River there is a wife and mother blessed with the divine touch, should she then be allowed to waste her skill upon her husband Tom and sister Carrie with occasionally Uncle Jack on Sundays? I think not. It is not fair to the rest of us nor yet to her. The artist must be given the widest possible scope in that field to which it has pleased God to call him. A woman who knows how to cook belongs in no man's home. She is very properly the servant of her public. Surely something would have been lost to the world had Wagner made his music for friends and relatives alone.

Perhaps we shall change our whole conception of home, at least on its physical side, and admit that it cannot compete with industry and that the processes carried on in it are for quite other reasons than efficiency. We no longer depend on fireplaces for heat or candles for lighting and yet we make use of them for their aesthetic and recreational values. It seems probably that the same thing may happen to other mechanical processes. It has happened to some extent already with cooking and sewing.

Even though we accept the fact that many processes now carried on in the home can be more efficiently carried on in the factory, we may nevertheless retain some of them for other reasons. While realizing that a bakery doughnut might score just as high and be made in much shorter time, we may continue to make doughnuts because we can put in just the amount of nutmeg that John likes and after all, we enjoy making doughnuts. Suiting the individual tastes of the family and recreation or at least pleasant work for ourselves are two very good reasons for making our own doughnuts though not the ones sometimes used today—the first duty of the housewife to do her own cooking and a possible money saving usually at a heavy cost in time and energy of the worker.

What then, will be our point of view? We will see the home as the place of abode of persons bound together by ties of affection, a place where affection of parents for one another, for their children, and among all members of the family is nurtured and enjoyed, where the immature are protected and guarded, a place where one may have rest and privacy, where one may keep his treasures, where one may satisfy his individual tastes, where fundamental culture consisting of customs, language, courtesies, and traditions, is conserved and passed on to the young, a place where altruism and other worthy character traits are generated and cultivated; a haven, a sanctuary, a source of inspiration, and a place where one may enjoy his individual kind of recreation and share it with others.

Our industrial age has brought more leisure and some economists believe that the best way to meet our large over production of goods followed by high powered salesmanship in an effort to dispose of these goods, is to have even shorter working days and shorter working weeks. This will mean even more leisure for the worker. In a recent article entitled "New Tools for Leisure," many suggestions were made for constructive leisure time activities that could well be practiced in the home—amateur writing, music, reading, large use of radio. The home could undoubtedly fill a much larger place as a recreational center than now, and I believe this is a problem for the home economist to consider.

Activities which contribute to any of these functions may well be retained. Too intangible for our matter-of-fact age, you may say. Yes, but there are distinct signs that our matter of fact age is finding itself unsatisfied with money and goods and more money and more goods and is seeking for values less tangible and appeals having more depth and significance. We have not yet determined the standard of living best suited to this industrial age in which we find ourselves today. When we do, it seems likely that intangible values will be included.

I believe that through the cultivation and enjoyment of human companionship and affection in family life, values heretofore only dimly sensed, can be found. Not only because of its biological foundation because it is a rich source of human enjoyment, the family will probably persist. Professor Ross has said, "It is likely that the public as it wins a deeper insight into the services of the family to society and to the race will feel less sympathy with the wrong-doings, weaknesses, and whims that shatter it."

What then of the future of home economics? For "to him that knoweth not the port to which he is bound no wind can be favorable." We need change our course only slightly. It will largely be a shifting of emphasis.

Some things very obviously we must do. We must be attentive to the discussions of the psychologist with his theories of human behavior that we may have help from him in solving behavior problems in the home, mental hygiene problems, problems of family adjustment. What of the new group calling themselves social psychologists? Have they answers to some of our problems of the home?

We must realize that the problems of homemaking cannot be solved by chemists alone, by physicists, by biologists. "Man does not live by bread alone" is as true today as when it was written, and "life is more than meat and the body than raiment." Not the physical, not the intellect alone, but one's emotions must be educated and controlled if life is to yield to us its highest prizes. Specialists in other fields have much, very much, to contribute but it is my conviction that once the foundations in fundamental subjects are laid, it is as women of fine intelligence, broad sympathy, imagination, scholarly standards, appreciation, and keen insight into the problems and possibilities of family life go out into related fields to seek specific help for specifically known needs that we shall be able to wrest from the specialized fields of knowledge those things most useful to homes.

We stand confused, almost confounded by the great complexity of life, the kaleidoscopic changes that our twenty years have seen. The mechanical, money-dominated age seems to leave us little choice; we are swept along at a pace too rapid to allow us any leisurely contemplation; we are overstimulated, hard pressed.

By and by, however, we shall learn to use more effectively the new tools which the industrial age has given us. We shall determine what mechanical tools are needed for satisfactory living in this technical age. It has come upon us so quickly that we have few measures of adequacy. Do we need a radio, an automobile, a telephone, even?

Out of all the bewildering cross-currents of our present social order we shall hope to salvage the home, changed in many aspects, but essentially the same—the institution most dear to all of us, yet the very center of the storm of unrest which is whipping society about so mercilessly, leaving in its wake one divorce for every seven marriages, broken homes of all sorts, children cheated of their right to be protected and to be surrounded by affection and understanding, restless persons seeking substitutes for families and home, substitutes which will allow them to be as self indulgent as they like. It is not a simple problem and it is bound up with the most vital issues of life itself. The home that emerges, the home economics that trains for this home is likely to be changed in many particulars though essentially the same. We need great wisdom if we are to recognize essentials and help to conserve them.

Home economics stands in a strategic position in that we should be able to bring together and weld into a powerful whole those constructive forces which make for wholesome human living. If we are wise, if we are discriminating, if we are courageous, we can serve our generation well by informing ourselves of the true situation, then seeking help from all the sources known to us—and they are many, and their keepers are generous and most of them as eager as we to put at the disposal of homekeepers all they have to give from the natural sciences, the social sciences, the arts.

I agree heartily with Dr. Ogburn when he says,

> The family will have to work out new adjustments to the small family, to a family with reduced production in the home for women, to a family which is not to be held together so much by economic and social bonds, but which is to be based on affection. To make these adjustments, the family will have to make new inventions and utilize new researches in the psychology of personality, utilize new knowledge regarding the habits and practices of affection, and the new discoveries regarding the training of children. It does not seem probable that the family will recover the functions it has lost. But even if the family doesn't produce thread and cloth and soap and medicine and food, it can still produce happiness, which does not seem such a very bad thing to do, after all.

I believe home economics is directing its course to such a port and that we are outward bound.

4

Trends in
Home Economics

Margaret M. Justin
President, American Home Economics Association

In presenting recent trends in home economics, it is impossible to disregard other developments which color and shape our progress in every line of education, particularly in the education of women. Home economics is not something simple, independent, separate, to be considered apart from its time, from other educational forces, or from the sociological, economic, and philosophic aspects of the day. Moreover, any attempt at analysis of trends requires that we know from whence we came, what sisters there be of our lineage, what hostages we have received at the hands of Dame Fortune, and whither we are bound.

Less than a century ago, the conventions of society and the educational system together held fast the idea that being a woman of itself limited the breadth, depth, and quality of the mind. It was commonly accepted that a girl had no abilities for any career besides that of housewife, and no need of training for that, except to learn through practice to do things economically, tastefully, and well so that she might contribute more largely to the comforts of her husband and his family, rear sons who would become leaders in the community, and daughters who, in their turn, would make other families comfortable. Much of this ability was deemed a matter of maternal instinct. The home was man's castle—woman's domicile.

Those interested in the problem of improving this situation in the education of women approached it in two ways. The first was to demonstrate that the abilities of woman are equal to those of man by competitive study of the same curricula as those pursued by men in the colleges from which women were excluded. The question as to whether the curriculum would function in the life of the individual woman was not raised—the universal acceptance of the classics as the "highway of learning" precluded such inquiry. The point at stake was to prove that woman had the breadth, depth, and quality of mind to carry a curriculum deemed through ages as cultural for man.

This step was taken with ease in the pioneer country where formal societal patterns were broken or lacking. The natural, unquestioned development and spread of coeducation in the frontier section was highly important in the whole movement of woman's education. It is significant that before the founding of any of the women's colleges, Oberlin, a college on the Ohio frontier, granted the first bachelor's degree to a woman.

By the time women's colleges in the east were organized and their long courageous struggle for the recognition of intellectual equality and the development of equal intellectual opportunity was well begun, the midwestern colleges, already coeducational, were adopting the second way of improving the status of women's education—launching the interesting venture of "applied" education. It was the belief of these educational pioneers that the prevalent classical education should and could be revised to fit a scheme of state-sponsored education so that the student's faculties might be developed not only to enrich his personal life and his participation in the social and civic life of the community but at the same time to provide for his vocational or professional training. With the promulgation of plans for educating the engineer, the architect, the agriculturist so that they might make a life and a living, a further innovation was urged. Homemaking came to be described as a profession requiring knowledge, techniques, and skills as definite as those required by the law, medicine, or engineering. This did not happen in a moment, or from one person or one school. Certain "advanced females" in the east, among them Catherine Beecher and her colleagues, had fomented the idea about the middle of the century. In 1873, just as the eastern women's colleges were coming into being, J. A. Anderson of the Kansas State Agricultural College presented plans for an education "precisely fitted to woman's needs" in the first college curriculum in home economics, then called "domestic economy," and established a department of sewing and courses in household chemistry.

Naturally, women in eastern colleges, struggling for recognition of equality of mental ability, saw danger in an education "precisely fitted for woman's work." Differentiation before recognition might be fatal to and would surely delay the long-sought victory. On the other hand, it is not surprising that women in the mid-west, accustomed to coeducation with its implication of full equality, should fail to understand the underlying causes for such a feeling. Moreover, distance, difficulties of communication, and sectional pride prevented intercourse in the general field of woman's education. The midwest states through their state colleges and universities became irrevocably committed to both coeducation and applied education. As a result of this difference in outlook, those fostering woman's education were divided into two camps, each inclined to accentuate differences and to become closed against the influence of the other. This situation inevitably effected the development of home economics.

Looking back over the early work in home economics, we see that it was little more colored by consideration of the needs of the individual than was the work in classical courses. It was largely colored by the current conception of the requirements of the job—as might be expected when a great effort was being made to develop a profession of homemaking on a par with the professions followed by men and with training of the same order. The profession of homemaking was complicated, its activities many and varied, and the skills required for the mechanics of housekeeping numerous. An attempt to meet the problems arising from the physical phases of homemaking led to the large number of college courses in breadmaking, laundering, and dressmaking that characterized the early work. Yet despite misplaced emphasis and many inadequacies, the idea of an education "precisely fitted to woman's needs" spread and took firm root.

Gradually, new departments were formed, graduate work began, and the work was extended down into the high and elementary schools. Extension of the work into the high school entailed an adjustment of the college curriculum which was not always successfully accomplished. Many soundly drawn curricula became through uncritical accretion literally "bogged down" with courses that did not carry skills and activities fundamental either to making life or yet to making a living. There was no clearing house, no chance for discussion among those trained for the work. Standards and requirements alike remained inchoate. Women were as yet scarcely aware of individual power and accomplishment and those working in home economics were not yet professionally conscious of the scope and influence of their field. Here and there was vision true. Many "could not see the wood for the trees," though here and there were persons of true vision. The men and women of the Lake Placid group, and notably their leader, Ellen H. Richards, brought to home economics the impetus of redirection and the strength of organization. Stereotypes of days long done were broken and provision made for new plans, new adventures, new growth. Strength through an organization, expression through a professional journal, and standards through the example of a fine scientific research attitude are part of their contribution. Mrs. Richards' direct contribution to home economics constitutes only part of our debt to her; she was able also to open to women opportunities for special study that, as we have seen during the last two decades, are continuing to enrich the whole field of women's education.

These last decades have also affected other regions of woman's world, perhaps none more markedly than our economic world. "Efficiency," "quantity production," "machine-made," have become commonplace terms that cover rather than disclose the assumption by the factory of former household skills. Bread-making, weaving, dairying, all have been largely taken from the home. Instead of home production, controlled by family wishes, women now face the task of making wise choice in many lines of commercial goods with its implied requirement of wide knowledge.

What effect is this having on curricula in home economics? The time once spent in courses furnishing skill and techniques must be replaced by courses which supply the broader knowledge, courses which afford an understanding of the economics of consumption and the responsibilities of the ultimate consumer. Of the activities remaining in the home, many that once were accomplished by human effort have been turned over to mechanical devices, and this entails the necessity for information concerning the efficiency, economy, and maintenance of such household equipment.

This economic reorganization also tends to lessen the need of the home for the services of its children so that the family faces the problem of carrying them as economic liabilities rather than as partial assets. This, in turn, raises problems in child training which are far-reaching. Closely connected with such problems is that of the increasing number of homemakers who are employed for either part or full time outside the home, a situation which is largely the result of the economic pressure attendant on our present high standard of living. Unless these problems are recognized and met family disorganization will result to an increasing degree.

The change in the economic activities of the home from those which combine production and consumption to those concerned chiefly with consumption is not the only great change that it has seen. Modern transportation and communication have cut the isolation in which the home formerly stood. It seems sometimes as if the societal forces which once played on it centripetally now are changed and tend to disperse rather than conserve its vitality.

From all this, however, we realize more and more clearly that of the tasks yet remaining in the home that of building human health and character is of chief and ever increasing importance. As Groves says in "Social Problems of the Family,"

> It is because of the significance of the child's first few years physically, mentally, socially, that society is so largely a product of family conditions. When the child leaves home to enter school he has already received a large part of the social influences coming out of his environment that determine character.

The understanding and acceptance of this has brought a greater change in home economics than in any other line of education. Courses in child development and in family relationships have been added; but more than this, there is a definite trend to ask regarding every part of the curriculum, "How does this help the individual to become an integrated personality, able to stand the physical, mental, and social stress of our time? How does this function for the betterment of homes?" Nothing could stimulate greater correlation and coordination of education in home economics than such inquiry.

Among the many other factors shaping home economics, there is yet one more on which I would touch, the change in the status of woman since home economics began. Within a quarter of a century, barriers, barricades, and pedestals alike have been washed out by the high tide of modern times. Today she may stand not militant, nor subservient, but adequately independent, vested in citizenship and social responsibility. Cognizance of this must be taken in her training if she is to understand currents and counter currents in her own life.

To provide for economic independence and develop an individual independence which may conserve interest in family life becomes a problem in woman's education. It is one that touches home economics most closely, since training in that profession leads to economic independence while cultivating interest in the home. As the field of home economics broadens, such opportunity is increased. We may count with pride the vocations open to home economics trained women, but I am confident that as yet we have only made a beginning of that which may be accomplished. Each new professional opportunity affects constructively the entire field.

What of tomorrow? Being neither seer nor prophet, I can only answer, "That depends on our today." Let us build in our best wisdom today, willing, like Kipling's builders in "The Palace," that the structure of our fashioning yield to the larger needs of tomorrow, and, like them, asking only to leave

> . . . . carven on every stone,
> "After me cometh a builder. Tell him, I, too, have known."

PART TWO

Refocusing on the Home and Family

1933 - 1959

The aim of homemaking education should be to improve family living, help families achieve their own goals, include all members of the family, develop abilities needed for democratic family living, contribute to satisfying personal life and to adjustment to social and economic environment, help in the development of fine communities, help people live better in the homes they have with what they have.

HOMEMAKING EDUCATION IN THE HIGH SCHOOL
Williamson and Lyle - 1954

5

New Frontiers in Home Economics Education

Frances Zuill

The future development of home economics offers an interesting subject for study and speculation. Even a superficial consideration of the economic and social forces that play upon the family in present-day society points out the complex problems that are involved in home and family life. So inter-related are our social institutions that problems of family life can scarcely be separated from those that pertain to industry, government, or school. It is no simple matter to determine what constitutes an adequate training for homemaking, even in homes that we know intimately, but it would truly take a crystal gazer of a new kind to predict the type of home economics that will play a significant role in the future.

In some ways the home and family have not kept pace with the rapid advances in other social institutions. Any fair cross-section of homes would show that modern machinery has not revolutionized homes in general as com-pletely as some writers would have us believe. Our association with homes in our own communities does not give us the same picture as do statistics. Changes in family housing, equipment, and methods of work have come somewhat slowly in comparison with similar changes in industry, partly because the home and family have not been subjected to the same searching inquiries that have been so commonly used in industry, and partly because the home is a very small unit operating for an entirely different kind of profit. Home economics is concerned with the type of home and family life that is best adapted to society as we find it and that will yield the maximum of satisfac-tion for the family, considering other conditions. Forward-looking movements in home economics will involve the whole environment and will be less con-fined by the walls of the home than formerly.

President Hoover's Committee on Social Trends in the United States finds that the family has "declined in social significance" in the past thirty years, "although not in human values." If home life is as important to national stability as sociologists have claimed, there is some evidence that a new program for family life is needed. The particular type of education or training that will help maintain the home as a significant unit in society is a difficult problem to contemplate, and the part of home economics in such a program is our chief concern.

It is interesting to note that the thirty-year period in which the family declined in importance coincides with the period of greatest progress in home economics. Does this fact have any meaning for us? Home economics was really established because social and economic conditions changed important functions in the family and created a need for a reconstructed type of family life. It is interesting to reflect about the vital contributions of home economics to family welfare during this thirty-year period. Has the nature of the work been such that it has helped the family to adjust to its different functions? Has there been too much of a tendency to assume responsibility for the sort of training that the family formerly assumed? What part has home economics had in maintaining the human values of which Mr. Hoover's committee speaks?

Up to this time home economists have not been credited with a very broad concept of education for family life. Whether this is a just criticism is not the question, but in looking ahead to a type of education that will play a significant part in the life of the family group and develop the personalities of the individuals in the group, it is important for us to re-examine our concept of homemaking. Perhaps too much time and emphasis have been given to traditional types of home economics, to activities that are not now socially useful, and that other more fundamental values have therefore been omitted. In the absence of comprehensive family studies, home economics education has been determined largely by opinions of specialists, and it is not strange if errors in judgment can be pointed out. It is much easier to deal with the realities of life than with abstractions. Perhaps this is one reason why home economics has dealt more effectively with home practices than with the other family functions that are of a more social and psychological nature.

That the future of home economics is dependent upon a better understanding of contemporary family life and a better adaptation of homemaking education to problems of the modern family, home economists are well aware. The need for a more critical and continuous study of family functions has been rather forcefully brought out during the depression. The effects of time and circumstance upon home life have been well illustrated. The influences of the outside world upon the family are constantly making further changes. Since there is little or nothing about family problems that is final, there must be a constant revaluation of the home economics program in terms of the basic values of life.

Let us consider some of the factors that have tended to limit our own perspective of homemaking. Customs, ideas, and attitudes built around family life are more difficult to change than those that are built around institutions with a less personal or human interest. Precedents set by previous generations, as well as by parents, neighbors, and friends, are strong influences in maintaining established home practices. Racial family customs are sometimes continued in entirely new environments. Then, too, there is a kind of loyalty to home and family that makes us resist certain types of change. This is well illustrated by food habits. How often home economists hear the statement, "But mother does it this way, and that's the way I like it." There are those who adopt new ideas for the home very reluctantly, although they utilize modern methods in business enterprises and stand for progressive movements in school and government. Because of such situations the family seems to lag in certain phases of its development and to change its standards more slowly. Limited home and family experiences are not conducive to a broad concept of homemaking.

In practically every discussion of plans for future developments in home economics education reference is made to the need for comprehensive studies of contemporary family life; yet the difficulties encountered in attempting to study families on any large scale are exceedingly well known. Some of the most important values in home life are almost impossible to measure objectively, and therefore there is a tendency to ignore them. Then, too, the problems involved in a homemaking program are exceedingly complicated.

However, the amount of attention that has been given to family problems recently has made available some valuable material in planning future work in home economics. I refer particularly to *Middletown*, to the reports of the White House Conference on Child Health and Protection and of the President's Conference on Home Building and Home Ownership, and also to reports of the President's committees on recent economic and social trends. A careful study of these gives a picture of home and family problems that is quite unlike that which one might get from a study of home economics courses or job analysis. A comparison of the findings of these reports with the content of some of our home economics courses would emphasize our shortcomings and point the way to progressive movements in our field. The contribution of some of our home economics leaders to the two conference reports is evidence of the progress that home economics has made in the fields of child welfare and housing, and it suggests the active part that all home economists should play in these and other phases of living.

It may be that lack of preparation for family life has been a factor in its decline in importance. A few weeks ago a Swiss home economics teacher who was visiting schools in this country commented upon the fact that many Americans do not consider homemaking an occupation worthy of training.

This is a very different attitude from that in her own small state of Zurich in Switzerland, where successful family life is considered of so much importance to their national security that a young woman must possess two things before she can marry: a homemaking certificate and a minimum of $600. Although family problems are exceedingly complex and homemaking is almost a universal occupation, there is in this country no widespread recognition of the value of special training for it. If homemaking is thought of as an occupation for women who merely cater to the physical needs of families, then one can understand why there are some who rely upon intuition instead of training. Social and psychological problems are not so easily answered by intuition.

Until the social significance of the family is more generally recognized and homemaking is thought of as a cooperative enterprise for men and women, preparation for family life will not be considered very essential. Not long ago, a well educated woman, the wife of a university professor, was discussing the marriage of a friend who had taken a doctor's degree in psychology. She expressed utter astonishment at her friend's interest in her home, her attention to household activities, as well as her willingness to do all of her own work with a baby in the house, and concluded by saying, "I just can't understand how she does it, because she has a very high I.Q." How well this illustrates the narrow concept of homemaking! To her, homemaking is a round of household drudgery with no other end in view. Is this the picture of home and family life that courses in home economics leave with "potential" homemakers? Do home economics courses challenge the intelligence of our students and create the type of interest in family problems that will lead to further study?

Our problem is one of re-focussing home economics for the future. For a considerable number of years, food and nutrition, textiles and clothing, and the various aspects of housing have been the pivots around which almost all of our subject matter has revolved. Of course, health, art, economics, sanitation, and management as they relate to the main pivotal subjects have been included. More recently family relationships has been added as a fourth pivot, but, judging from the amount of time and attention devoted to this in the school systems, it does not occupy an equally important position.

I have had a feeling for a long time that this organization of subject matter has tended to narrow our conception of homemaking by centering attention upon three essential phases of living, all of which deal with the physical needs of individuals. I am convinced that any over-emphasis upon household activities which are related to food preparation, clothing construction, and care of the house is a direct result of centering so much attention upon these three subjects. They represent three physical needs of human beings, but they are a part of consumer-producer education. They rightfully belong in a study

47

of the economic function of the family. A school official, in defending his method of cutting school costs, recently said, "It is well enough to teach foods and clothing in prosperous times, but these children live in families where they have to get the most they possibly can with little money that is available." To him there was not the slightest connection between home economics and the consumer problems which these families faced in their daily living. Food, nutrition, textiles, and housing are not separate from consumer problems— they are consumer problems.

If we centered our attention upon the important functions of the family instead of upon subjects, we would not only do a better job in preparing for family life, but we would give to the public a clearer idea of what home economics is attempting to do. It is natural that young inexperienced teachers of home economics should find difficulty in keeping homemaking in mind as the ultimate goal when the main emphasis in their training seemed to have been on subject matter. It takes maturity and experience to relate our ideas of family life and our ideas of education and to unite them in a philosophy of homemaking education. An elderly man who is overseer of the poor in a small Iowa community, in speaking of the relief activities of the home economics teacher, said, "She knows her subjects, but she doesn't know much about living."

Many home economics teachers have adapted their courses to the needs of their communities during the depression. A report of home economics projects bearing on relief activities has been compiled by the Office of Education and has been published as Circular No. 84. But we must not let the present obscure the future. Only a few will revert back to the older types of home economics when normal times return. I feel that this will be the beginning of an important reorganization period in home economics work. I believe that family functions will be the basis on which courses are reorganized. I predict that the important family functions will be the focus of attention instead of subject matter. Do we not all admit that the primary aim of home economics is to enable boys and girls to perform effectively the functions of the family, whether as individuals or members of the group? If this is true, why not approach the subject from this angle?

It is not the purpose of this paper to discuss in detail the social, psychological, and economic functions of the family. A few illustrations will help to clarify the argument, however. Everyone realizes that now the important economic function of the family is as consumer rather than as producer, and that problems of consumption have increased as production in the home has diminished; but an examination of our courses shows that consumption is considered as the "by-product" and that the approach is indirect instead of direct. It is obvious that in preparing goods for use in the family the homemaker is a producer, and this may be equally true of the services she

48

renders to the family. The increase in consumption probably represents a fairly permanent change in the economic functions of the family. In challenging a similar statement a home economist cited the present increase in such productive activities as home canning, bread baking, and home sewing, but this increase probably illustrates a response to a crisis rather than a return to the old order and is comparable to our war-time work. This incident shows the tendency we have to defend productive activities in home economics courses. A limited number of useful productive activities in home economics courses need no defense, for they will no doubt continue as a part of the work of the home in many cases. They remain as a part of the economic function of the family, even if they occupy a position of minor importance. It is not because productive activities should be eliminated, but because they should occupy their proper place in the home that we call attention to the decline in their importance. They have in the past submerged other functions.

In focussing attention upon the economic function of the family, the importance of sound nutrition principles, marketing information, and principles of food preparation should in no way be minimized. Certainly wise consumption of food is based upon a knowledge of these subjects and an intelligent application of them on planning and purchasing. These subjects would be taught as thoroughly as ever but as a means to wise consumption, so that health and other objectives may be realized. This is just to illustrate the change in emphasis. Subject matter courses in textiles and clothing as well as housing would be taught from the standpoint of consumer education rather than as ends in themselves. Satisfaction in the use of goods and appreciation of art in household goods are as truly consumer problems as quality, quantity, or price.

The social and psychological functions of the family are as important as the economic function. It is even more interesting to speculate about the part that home economics should play in the future in training for these two functions. Only five years ago we shied away from this responsibility, but progressive courses no longer fail to consider the aspects of child care and training, personality development, character education, and family stability that are adapted to the age of the students. Again let me emphasize that if these subjects are approached from the standpoint of family functions they will not be taught as ends in themselves, but as a means to more satisfactory social adjustment or personality development. What would be included in home economics courses in regard to environment, social aspects of housing, leisure time activities, and management if our courses emphasized family functions? What would happen to courses in family relationships and child care if they were permeated by a clear idea of the social function of the family?

In one type of curriculum construction which is very familiar to all of us, much emphasis is placed upon an analysis of home activities in which homemakers and their daughters participate. Does this method insure preparation for all the important family functions, or is the emphasis mainly on production and consumption? Can the psychological and social functions be studied by this method? Does this theory of curriculum research point the way to new developments in home and family life, or does it follow established practices? How does it take account of the lag in the home and the effect of parental attitudes? Does a study of women's activities in the home provide a suitable basis for homemaking as a cooperative enterprise? Many studies of home activities have been made and used in turn as an index for the selection of curriculum material. If the fundamental values of family life are what we are working toward, we need to re-evaluate the curriculum theories that have been most commonly used in home economics because the curriculum determines in a large measure what is actually taught in home economics. Whether or not home economics plays an important part in preparation for family life depends upon its new frontiers.

If it were possible to lay aside all preconceived notions in regard to home economics education and to think only of the environment that would insure the best development of the members of the family and provide the most satisfying home life, what type of home economics would you propose? A new program for home economics is just ahead.

6

Charting Our Future

Ivol Spafford

Dr. Spafford of Rock Creek, Ohio, has accepted the responsibility of writing the report of the AHEA committee on criteria for evaluating college programs of home economics. She was curriculum director of the General College at the University of Minnesota from 1935 to 1940 and was with the Alabama Department of Education from 1919 to 1934.

Home economics developed out of a concern for the betterment of home and family living. Basically that concern has controlled its development. Home economics teaching in elementary and high school is, and should be, directed largely toward increasing satisfactions in personal and family living and in raising the level of family living. It should not be overlooked, however, that the learning we value most in high school home economics for its long-time personal and family life values has worth in the larger community and that some of it offers specific preparation for certain types of wage-earning jobs open to high school students.

The same opportunity for improving family life exists in home economics teaching at the college level. All home economists would agree that college graduates in home economics should be our most successful family members in their present families, also our most successful homemakers when they marry. College home economics offers the added opportunity, for those who desire it, to prepare for wage earning in vocations that stem from a concern for the affairs of the home and the family.

Changes in home economics have come about largely through changes in the social situation, on the one hand, and through the acquisition of new knowledge and new experiences on the other. As we examine our individual home economics programs, we see much of worth in what we have done and are doing. If we look critically, we are aware of many places at which we fall short of putting into practice the best of what we know.

Our strengths at the high school level lie largely (1) in a broadening of the scope of our program, (2) in the increasing number we are reaching, (3) in our willingness to teach all students regardless of their academic ability, and (4) in our desire to deal with real situations and to have pupils use their learning in their daily living. The most serious weaknesses in our high school teaching lie in an underemphasis on values in life and on human relationships and an overemphasis on the material aspects of living.

Little can be said in regard to our strengths in the first six years of schooling. A few elementary schools with or without our help are definitely interested in education for home and family life. During recent years, we have become concerned that adequate and functional nutrition instruction be given during these early years and we have endorsed and promoted a school lunch feeding program. That is the limit of our general concern for the home life education of children from 6 to 12 years of age.

Our strengths at the college level lie largely (1) in extending the scope of subject-matter content, (2) in increasing the emphasis on social and economic aspects, and (3) in improving the quality and extent of our preparation for wage earning. Our most serious weaknesses in colleges as a whole are our unwillingness to accept preparation for home and family living as the first concern of a college home economics department and our failure to extend our leadership and our offerings toward making such preparation a major objective of the total institution for all its students. We are also to be criticized for our limited use of experimental and research techniques in building our program and in appraising our success in achieving what we say we are trying to do.

Our Acts Today Shape Our Future

Every thoughtful person knows that we are living in a world of confusion. Violence in group and personal relationships surrounds us. People with quite different beliefs as to human values are striving for places of leadership. Although we have an abiding faith in democracy, if we are honest with ourselves we know that few of us have learned to live it in all our relationships.

This failure to live democratically concerns all of us in a democracy. It is of special concern to home economists, for it is in part a measure of the success or failure of our teaching. The degree to which we achieve the democratic way of life in our total society and in all our relationships depends largely upon how well we live and teach democracy in the home. As we face this fact, we must also face the fact that the number of broken homes is increasing.

The situation is more serious today than ever before because of changes in the world as a whole. Whatever happens in the furthermost outposts means something to us today. The increasing emphasis on material things—the newest gadgets, the latest clothes and furnishings—and a life without serious purpose are dangerous trends.

Some people say that confusion as to values and a spirit of recklessness and selfishness always follow war. These things are rather a part of what leads to war. And neither war nor an attitude that things will eventually work themselves out will cause people to substitute other more permanent values. It is not too late to achieve richness of life for all people and an accompanying peace. We shall achieve it, however, only as we put our faith in democracy wholeheartedly to work in our living and in our teaching.

The need for a satisfying and fulfilling home life is greater than ever before—and this is true at every age level. The individual needs to feel that he counts in the life of someone. He needs the opportunity to give and receive affection. He needs a place where he can be himself. The successful home provides these values for its members from infancy to old age.

The home serves also as an educational institution. The child's first learning takes place there. His ideals of human relationships, his set of values, his attitudes and appreciations, his habits of living and working have their foundation in early home experiences. Learning in the home, however, does not stop with early childhood. People continue to learn throughout life from their experiences in the home and with the family as well as their experiences elsewhere. Learning within the home will have its greatest personal and social value as it is thoughtfully guided by people who have themselves given thought to the worth of these experiences and who have learned how to make the most of them both for themselves and for others.

Our Job Ahead Is Clear

For those home economists who believe that our major concern is to educate for successful home and family living, the job ahead is clear. We must first of all bend our personal efforts to achieving a life that is rich and fruitful in its everyday living.

For those home economists whose job is teaching—and teaching is done in many places other than the classroom—a second responsibility exists. We must seek to help those we teach to develop worth-while and attainable ideals for today's world for themselves and their families and for society as a whole. We must also so direct our teaching that the attainment of these ideals is accompanied by the attainment of the necessary attitudes and appreciations, techniques and habits for achieving them in life itself.

As we chart our future, we must re-examine our entire program. Such an appraisal should begin with a critical study of our philosophy of life and of education, the goals we have set for our work, the practices we are using to achieve these goals, and our success in achieving them. Each program in the end must stand or fall on its own merits. We are not judged in real life by what a general and vague "home economics" believes or does not believe, does or does not do, but by what we as individuals and as specific home economics departments believe and do.

Colleges Hold the Key

Colleges hold the key to the future of home economics. Only as they see clearly and do well their job can home economics reach its full possibilities. By and large, college men and women should be our best homemakers, our most social-minded young people, our strongest believers and practicers of democracy. With a program of home and family life education provided as an integral part of their general education, whether they be home economics majors or not, we should expect to have top-flight performers in all these aspects of living. Leadership in interesting an institution in such a program and the responsibility for seeing that the program is broad and functional rests squarely on us.

Through the professional training in home economics which they offer, colleges have both the responsibility and the opportunity to influence the thinking as to goals and methods of achievement of the total home economics program. Important in charting the future of college home economics is the work of AHEA's committee on criteria for evaluating college programs of home economics. This committee has set for itself the task of providing criteria by which an institution may evaluate its own program. Accompanying these criteria will be descriptive material which deals with the point of view of committee members in regard to the characteristics of good college departments, also examples of ways in which departments are carrying out their programs. Values in this study will depend largely upon the use made of it by individual colleges and departments of home economics.

7

The Philosophy of the Early Home Economists

Lita Bane

The late Lita Bane, who served the American Home Economics Association as executive secretary, vice-president, and president, had a distinguished career in home economics in Extension Service, journalism, teaching, and administration.

This article was first published in The Kitchen Reporter, *published by Kelvinator Kitchen, Detroit, in September 1953. It is reprinted in this anniversary issue of the* Journal *with the permission of the Kelvinator Division of American Motors Corporation.*

Our times set such a fast pace that we sometimes find ourselves a little confused about our directions. It is then that a look at landmarks may help to set us back on the road with our confidence as well as our sense of direction restored—hence this excursion into the past for a look at the philosophy of our home economics pioneers.

The serious consideration of home economics as a specialized area of study began with the Lake Placid Conferences held annually from 1899 through 1908. It is in the reports of these conferences that we find the basic philosophy upon which home economics has been built. That household arts are important to the home had long been realized. The possibilities of making use of the findings of science in homemaking were emerging—the idea of giving students an insight into the vital importance of homemaking to society as a whole was new. And the idea that all of this might be incorporated into formal education was quite revolutionary!

Accomplishments of Early Conferences

The hope that something might be done about establishing homemaking courses at various levels of education brought together 11 people in response to the invitation of the board of trustees of the Lake Placid Club, who believed that the time was "ripe for some united action on this sociologic problem." Mr. and Mrs. Melvil Dewey acted as host and hostess for the conferences. Mr. Dewey was secretary of the University of the State of New York and director of the New York State Library. It was his belief that those who can make the home all it should be will contribute more to the basic needs of life than even teachers, ministers, and editors. And his wife stated as her belief that the things of the spirit, the invisible forces which make men great, are developed by education, evolution, sound judgment and constructive measures—and that the supreme factor in such development is the home.

The importance of the home to the individual and to society was often stressed in these early meetings and, it is interesting to note, the term "home economics" was used at the very first meeting. Mental health was mentioned also, as well as the importance of a rational division of the family income and better home management.

The momentum of any movement does not always depend upon the number of interested people—as we well know. In this instance, 11 people attended the first conference and 76 attended nine years later (just as the conference was becoming the American Home Economics Association). . . . Their faith might have been strained a little had they been asked to believe then that in a matter of 50 years there would be an organization of some 25,000 members with constitution, bylaws, and a home of its own in the nation's capital! . . .

Quotes of Early Leaders

I have always favored letting people speak for themselves. And so I am going to quote some of our pioneers. To me, many of their ideas sound up to date and timeless—as they probably will to you.

We would start, I suppose, with Ellen H. Richards. I found it difficult to choose from the many significant things she said. The gist of her philosophy, however, can be found in her statement, "Control the material things which lie about you and make natural and social forces do your bidding, in order that you may have time and energy to make life beautiful and gracious and worthwhile."

Her definition of what home economics should represent is so important I cannot refrain from repeating it, familiar as it must be to you. Home economics, she says, should stand for:

The freedom of the home from the dominance of things and their due subordination to ideals.
The utilization of the resources of modern science to improve home life.

The simplicity in material surroundings which will free the spirit for the more important and permanent interests of the home and of society.
The ideal home life for today unhampered by the traditions of the past.

She was a chemist, but she had interests far beyond the field of chemistry.

Marion Talbot was for a long time professor of household administration and dean of women at the University of Chicago. Earlier she had collaborated with Mrs. Richards in writing a book on home sanitation. She always emphasized the social responsibility of the home. "Home Economics," she said, "must always be regarded in the light of its relation to the general social system. Men and women alike are concerned in understanding the processes, activities, obligations, and opportunities which make the home and the family effective parts of the social fabric."

Dr. W. O. Atwater is another name familiar to home economists, both because of his original research in the field of nutrition and the work of his daughter, Helen, who was editor of the *Journal of Home Economics* for many years. Being one of the first scientists to point out the importance of nutrition (both to the individual and to the general welfare), he urged the need for more research in order that we might know what foods and what methods of preparing them furnish the most economical and healthful diet. He believed one of our fundamental problems was to find out how national food production could be made to yield better returns in economic and social progress and social welfare.

Isabel Bevier, the second president of the American Home Economics Association, believed that home economics has an opportunity to teach something of the beauty of life and the unity of life, to teach that there is an art in a well-ordered home and a well-ordered life, and that "perhaps that is the greatest thing home economics has to do." She stood for many things, but probably the one having the most far-reaching influence was her conviction that "home economics must stand, first of all, for sound scholarship."

The list is long—so rich is our background in constructive ideas, fine ideals and high standards. Many names appear in the early records—names we recall with appreciation . . .

Objectives of Home Economics

If I were to gather into a few statements the ideas that seem to me to have been most powerful in shaping the philosophy underlying the home economics movement, they would be:

Utilization of modern science to improve home life
Study of the humanities with the same objective
Sound scholarship always
Research in order to add to the sum of reliable information

Use of all resources to make home and family life effective parts of the social fabric

Constant emphasis upon the ultimate purpose of controlling the material things and making natural and social forces do our bidding

. . . An opportunity for creativeness and self-expression in home living has from the first been one of the prime objectives of home economics. When I was writing these paragraphs, I was reminded of . . . Caroline L. Hunt, another of our pioneers, [and] her inspiring words: "The final test of teaching home economics is freedom. If we have unnecessarily complicated a single life by perpetuating useless conventions or by carrying the values of one age over into the next, just so far have we failed. If we have simplified one life and released in it energy for its own expression, just so far have we succeeded."

Philosophy is Inspiring

After reading the philosophy expressed by our early home economists, I always feel that I have allowed a refreshing breeze to blow through the confused thinking that the pressures of our day force upon us. The way ahead for home economists seems clearly indicated by the landmarks of the past. Ways and means change, but the fundamental human needs met by homes and families are much the same from age to age.

Encouragement for all of us is found in two sentences appearing at the end of a committee report made in 1900 at the Lake Placid Conference—"The way is long but the end is not uncertain. If the work we are attempting is in line with the great social and industrial forces of the day, its accomplishment (not necessarily in this form, but certainly in its main features) must be inevitable." . . .

The years have proved that the value placed by early home economists on "an intelligent mind and a trained hand" has been in the direct line of progress.

58

8

For Effective Teaching
of Family Living

Mary Lee Hurt and Ruth J. Dales

Dr. Hurt is chairman of home economics education at Michigan State University, and Dr. Dales is a professor of home and family life at the Florida State University.

Home economics teachers feel confident in teaching family living courses when they are equipped with the latest findings from research in the field and have ability to use methods and materials most suitable for accomplishing desired goals. Such evidence has been found by the authors in working with home economics teachers through workshops, short courses, and in-service education, and from follow-up evaluations with them at various intervals.

Purposes of Courses in Family Living

Through family living courses in schools, we may hope to accomplish two main purposes. The first of these relates to helping the adolescent understand himself, his own set of attitudes and values, and how they may be similar to or different from those of others. He learns to establish more satisfying relationships as he grows in his personal understanding as well as the understanding of friends and family members at their various stages in the life cycle. The second purpose we may hope to accomplish is to help the adolescent develop various approaches for clarifying and solving his own problems. No person meets the same problem in the same way twice during life. The role of education is to help the adolescent understand the steps in the problem-solving method and to evaluate effectiveness and fallacies in thinking through his problems. Sensitivity to his own values and attitudes will help him understand the alternatives possible in any problem-solving situation and to choose the alternative which will give greatest satisfaction to himself and others.

Important to Understand Students

The first requisite in teaching a family living course is to know and to understand the student group. Each student brings to class a set of attitudes and values about what is a "good" family, roles of family members, and the family in relation to other groups. He also has definite feelings about the pattern followed within his own family. Because regions—whether rural or urban—have varying ethnic groups and social class subcultures, the teacher of family living needs to study both the community and the prevalent patterns within families. A good teacher has many ways at her finger tips for studying her students and the family patterns in her community.

As a background she may find much help from reviewing literature in the field of sociology which describes social class and ethnic patterns of family life. Both Hollingshead (1) and Duvall (2) are excellent sources for information of this kind.

Awareness of changing peer relationships and codes of behavior during the adolescent years is needed by the understanding teacher. Careful listening and observation are leads for the alert teacher in keeping up to date in relation to these typically adolescent behaviors. Knowing what might be expected as normal maturity at different age levels is pertinent material for a teacher to have in helping the adolescent judge his own maturation level. There are many fine current studies on adolescence which would help a teacher refresh herself, such as those by Jersild (3), Kuhlen (4), Landis (5), Remmers (6), and Strang (7).

As a help in becoming acquainted with her class group, the teacher may use written forms to gain insight into the lives and families of the varied personalities with whom she will be working. More formal questionnaires may be used for information about the homes and families of her students, or open-ended questions may be asked as more revealing of attitudes and feelings toward families and others. Such topics might be, "What I do with my spare time," "Things I like to do best with girl or boy friends," "How our family celebrates special occasions," "How our family settles disagreements." The alert teacher will find she may learn much from observing her students in various situations and listening to them both in and outside of class.

Another requisite for understanding her students is an awareness of the developmental level of her adolescent group. An effective course in family living is based on the present and near future concerns and needs of the members of the class group. Concerns and needs of adolescents vary within any group. The teacher, in studying the family patterns in the community and the developmental tasks met by her students, will know whether they are ready for study of units in "brother-sister and parent relationships," "friendships," "dating," or "courtship and marriage." A number of check lists have been developed which may easily give her this information. Some of these are "The Mooney Problem Check List" *(8)* "Remmers SRA Youth Inventory" *(9)*, "Dales' Problem Check List" *(10)*, and "Problems in Personal and Family Living Checklist," which is available at Michigan State University *(11)*.

Assessment of the problems of older adolescents by experienced teachers over the last several years seems to indicate that the following are some of the most commonly selected areas for study: "Understanding Ourselves and Others," "Understanding Our Families," "Looking Toward Marriage Someday," "Establishing a Home of Our Own," "Management for Personal and Family Living," "The Children in Our Future," "The Family in the Community." One of the most recent sources in this field is "Living in Families" by the Smarts *(12)*.

Subject Matter Needed

The teacher in family living needs to have a sound understanding of the ׳family life cycle, the developmental needs of each family member in each stage of the cycle, and the effect of current forces in society upon the family. Thorough understanding of basic human needs and the various ways people find for meeting these needs, both for satisfaction and dissatisfaction to themselves and others, is essential background knowledge. The adolescent becomes more accepting of family situations when he understands the stage of the cycle in which his family may be at a particular time. If he is the youngest of several children and the only one yet at home, he may understand the overprotectiveness of his parents if he realizes the problems faced at the time of the "launching stage." Or, a grandfather who has just retired and no longer has an identity in the work world may present real problems in his family. The adolescent may be helped to understand his grandfather's point of view in this situation.

Expectations toward roles of family members vary from family to family. The teacher needs to be sensitive to the variations in these roles—especially those represented by the students in her class. It is very important to know the expectations for the adolescent by the family. For example, in some families the teen-age daughter could be expected to pattern after the mother and to help with all the household tasks before and after school. Yet, in another family she may be expected to obtain a job as early as possible and to begin to support herself and contribute to the family budget.

Creative Teaching for Effective Learning

Teaching will be effective when each area of study is introduced at the "teachable moment" for the majority of the students in the class. Also the good teacher not only uses varied methods effectively but understands why they are effective in making application of the principles of learning.

Attitudes and values so important in becoming a more effective person and family member are "caught not taught." Through association with others, one acquires these attitudes and values. In the classroom, learning situations should be provided for students to become associated with persons who might be able to influence them—such as the character in the story, the film, the playlet or sociodrama, or a person who is brought in as a speaker.

The family living teacher today needs to be aware of the environment which is influencing the adolescent's attitudes and behavior. She needs to keep abreast of local television programs and movies popular with this age group; with magazines for youth, such as *Seventeen* and *Compact*. Much fruitful discussion may be based on incidents portrayed through these media. Simple case situations and playlets may be developed by the teacher or students providing "springboards" for worthwhile discussions. Besides these playlets there are those published by the American Theater Wing *(13)* and the "Socioguidramas" *(14)*. Each year there is an increasing number of films and filmstrips available in this field through the various audiovisual centers *(15)*. Bulletin and flannel board displays aid in stimulating interest in the study of various phases of the subject.

Making Discussion Lessons Worthwhile

Many opportunities need to be provided for students to explore their varied concerns through guided discussion. In working with teachers, the authors have found that one of the teachers' greatest needs is the ability to lead effective problem-solving discussions and also to help students gain this ability. Teachers need real help in knowing how to clarify pertinent problems with adolescents; how to help them use all resources, both printed and personal, in securing all the facts related to the problem; how to develop the various alternatives, with all their consequences, for solving a problem, and helping them choose and evaluate a solution. There are times when a student group needs to end its discussion with the possible alternatives and consequences and let each student choose the one which best fits his own family and cultural background. Most questions discussed have no "right" or "wrong" answers but need application in many different patterns of family living.

Through discussions, students have an opportunity to test their own ideas and through listening to views of others within the group become more understanding and accepting of differing points of view, feelings, and attitudes. Worthwhile discussions need careful preparation both by the teacher and the students. Upon clarification of the problem the group needs to feel the importance of studying all the facts and views available as a basis for the discussion. Students may, individually or working in groups, study what the various references available have to offer about each subject and may present their findings as panels or symposiums. Resource people from the school or community may also be invited to provide necessary information. A teacher needs to encourage students to be careful in making statements which cannot be supported and to teach them to be scientific in their thinking *(16, 17, 18)*.

Counseling Ability Needed

Whenever a teacher attempts to offer a family living class she needs to have help in handling individual counseling situations. She needs to be sensitive to the unsolved problems of students within her group and to find ways to provide individual help for these students, either through her own counseling or referral to others.

Also a teacher of family living needs to recognize that problems may arise from her group which she feels inadequate to handle. At all times she needs to seek the counsel of her administrator in relation to the content of the course. He can be invaluable support in giving suggestions in relation to consultant help available in the community when needed.

In Summary

The effective teacher of family living needs to gain all the help and experience possible to develop her understanding of human behavior, appreciation of families, their differences and similarities at various stages of the family cycle; to keep abreast of the increasing literature and research in the field, the latest methods and materials; to be aware of the developing adolescent in today's changing culture; and to increase her understanding of, and ability to relate to, the youth of this age group. When home economics teachers have had help through in-service education in attaining these competences they feel more secure and assured and are able to provide invaluable help for adolescents who are growing to be "understanding and effective family members."

References

1. Hollingshead, A. *Elmtown's Youth.* New York: John D. Wiley & Sons, Inc., 1959.

2. Duvall, E. M. *Family Development.* Chicago: J. B. Lippincott Company, 1957.

3. Jersild, A. T. *Psychology of Adolescence.* New York: The Macmillan Company, 1957.

4. Kuhlen, R. G. *Psychology of Adolescent Development.* New York: Harper & Brothers, Publishers, 1952.

5. Landis, J. T., and M. G. *Building a Successful Marriage.* Englewood Cliffs, New Jersey: Prentice-Hall, Inc., 1958.

6. Remmers, H. H., and Radler, D. H. *The American Teenager.* New York: Bobbs-Merrill Company, Inc., 1957.

7. Strang, R. *The Adolescent Views Himself.* New York: McGraw-Hill Book Company, Inc., 1957.

8. Mooney, R. L. Problem Check List, Junior High School Form. Bureau of Educational Research, Ohio State University, Columbus, Ohio, 1950.

9. Remmers, H. H. SRA Youth Inventory. Science Research Associates, Chicago, 1949.

10. Dales, R. J. A method for measuring developmental tasks: scales for selected tasks at the beginning of adolescence. *Child Devel.* 26, No. 2 (June 1955), pp. 111-122.

11. Problems in Personal and Family Living Checklist, Bureau of Educational Research, College of Education, Michigan State University, East Lansing, 1953.

12. Smart, R., and M. S. *Living in Families.* Boston: Houghton Mifflin Company, 1958.

13. American Theater Wing Plays, National Association of Mental Health, 1790 Broadway, New York.

14. Socio-Guidramas Series, Occu-Press, 489 5th Avenue, New York.

15. Morgan, M., Goodson, N., and Gould, F. List of Films on Family Relations and Child Development. American Home Economics Association, Washington D. C., 1957.

16. Goller, G. Family life education. *Adult Leadership* 7, No. 4 (Oct. 1958), pp. 96-98.

17. Holmquist, D. Personal and family living in the school curriculum. *Delta Kappa Gamma Bulletin* 24, No. 4 (Fall 1958), pp. 19-27.

18. Luckey, E., and Neubeck, G. What are we doing in marriage education? *Marriage & Family Living* 18, No. 4 (Nov. 1956), pp. 349-354.

9

The Committee on Philosophy and Objectives

Dorothy D. Scott
Chairman, Committee on Philosophy and Objectives of Home Economics

The year 1959 marks the first half century of the American Home Economics Association. Three years ago, in preparation for the fiftieth anniversary, Association President Catherine T. Dennis appointed a committee to review the past, survey the present, and make suggestions for the future.

As the committee reviewed the past fifty years of home economics, we found that far more had been accomplished than the founders would have dreamed possible. We believe they would be proud of the progress made in carrying out the aims for home economics they set forth in 1909: ". . . to improve the conditions of living in the home, the institutional household, and the community." A number of achievements of the profession are listed in this statement. Some are a continuing part of the present and future.

In our survey of the present, we have considered the social changes growing out of the educational, scientific, and technological advances of the past fifty years; advances which have brought about profound changes in the home and in familiar patterns of family life—calling for a new order of emphasis on meeting family needs and wants.

However, we firmly believe that the underlying philosophy and basic tenets of the founders still apply and must guide new directions for the profession.

Many people have contributed to this statement. We hope it will bring to those outside the profession a better understanding of what home economics is, what it does, and of the many ways in which it contributes to the common good.

We believe it will sharpen the home economist's perception of the challenges and opportunities in the years ahead.

What Is Home Economics?

Home economics is the field of knowledge and service primarily concerned with strengthening family life through:

- educating the individual for family living
- improving the services and goods used by families
- conducting research to discover the changing needs of individuals and families and the means of satisfying these needs
- furthering community, national, and world conditions favorable to family living

Home economics synthesizes knowledge drawn from its own research, from the physical, biological, and social sciences and the arts and applies this knowledge to improving the lives of families and individuals. Its concern is with these aspects of family living:

- family relationships and child development
- consumption and other economic aspects of personal and family living
- nutritional needs and the selection, preservation, preparation, and use of food
- design, selection, construction, and care of clothing, and its psychological and social significance
- textiles for clothing and for the home
- housing for the family and equipment and furnishings for the household
- art as an integral part of everyday life
- management in the use of resources so that values and goals of the individual, the family, or of society may be attained

Though home economics is not the only professional field dealing with one or more of these aspects of living, it is the only field concerned with all of them, with their interrelationships, and with the total pattern which they form. It is the only field concerned with helping families shape both the parts and the whole of the pattern of daily living. The emphases that it gives to various aspects of living are determined by the needs of individuals and families in the social environment of their time.

Home economics prepares professional personnel to carry out its objectives through education, research, social welfare and public health, dietetics and institution administration, and business. It works co-operatively with other fields of education but assumes a unique responsibility for helping girls and boys, women and men, to achieve wholesome, happy lives. It shares with other fields the responsibility for developing perceptive, well-informed citizens with the ability and the will to further conditions favorable to effective living.

The Home Economics Profession Today

When the American Home Economics Association was established in 1909, the founders had only a few scattered educational programs in secondary schools and in the young land-grant colleges through which to carry forward their program of education for living. They could count only 700 persons ready to set a new direction through a national association. Yet, they dared to venture forth. Drawing on the meager educational programs of the day, they joined forces to help families improve the quality of their living.

If, today, our needs seem more complex than theirs, it is also true that we have far more knowledge and experience with which to chart the future of our profession.

Home Economics Today

... *in education*

Home economics is taught in school systems the length and breadth of the United States. It has an established place in nearly 500 colleges and universities.

Through public and private schools and such state and federally sponsored programs as the Cooperative Extension Service and Vocational Education programs, millions of adults and youth obtain formal and informal education for better living. Through many communications media, home economists provide education for families.

... *in research*

The findings of home economics research are widely disseminated and benefit homes in the United States and throughout the world. Research is conducted by the Institute of Home Economics of the U. S. Department of Agriculture, by home economics departments of state agricultural experiment stations, by other government agencies, by private agencies, by many colleges and universities, and by industry.

... *in business*

Many areas of business or commerce serving homes and families employ home economists. It is their responsibility to provide the link through which consumer needs are interpreted to industry and through which, in turn, families are assisted in the efficient use of products and services.

... *in dietetics and institution administration*

In hospitals and other institutions for group living, in restaurants, school lunch programs and industry, the health of millions is safeguarded and improved by the work of specialists in institution administration, nutritionists, dietitians, and other home economists engaged in food service.

. . . in social welfare and public health

Social welfare and public health agencies of the federal government and the states, of counties and cities, employ home economists. Many others are with voluntary agencies. Home economists with the federal government serve with such agencies as the Public Health Service, the Children's Bureau, and the Bureau of Public Assistance.

. . . in international service

International agencies of the United States and of the United Nations which contribute to health, welfare, and education programs use the services of home economists in all parts of the world. Home economists from abroad and those preparing to be home economists in their native countries come to study in the colleges and universities of this country.

Home Economics and Today's Families

A profession today must be willing—and equipped—to recognize and be guided by change and to relate its research and other activities to change. This is particularly true of home economics; it can be effective only as it alleviates the stresses and promotes the satisfactions brought about by new situations.

Home economists must be among the first to anticipate and recognize change, to weigh the capacities of the individual to meet new demands, and to set new directions for professional programs of benefit to families.

People will always find satisfaction in living to the extent that they can deal with their needs and with the circumstances of their times. Before we as a profession can coordinate knowledge and effort for the benefit of today's families, we must understand the times and the circumstances of their lives.

Comparing today's world with the world of fifty years ago, it is easy to identify a dozen or more fundamental changes which demand new capacities on the part of family members. These changes require vision and intelligence from those professions created to help families.

Consider, for example, the effect on the home and community of industrialization, urbanization and suburbanization, working mothers and commuting fathers, population growth, the increasing number of elderly people, the higher level of education, the shorter work week. Consider also the effect of the family's shift from a producing to a consuming unit; the interchanging roles of family members; greater awareness of the importance of the affectional function of the family; automation in the household; instantaneous communication and lightning-swift travel.

Each of these changes—and one could name others—has become an accepted and continuing trend within the lifetime of many of today's homemakers and within the lifetime of home economics. Changes of the future may transform our lives even more quickly. The fact of change is seen more clearly than its form. What are the knowledges and skills that will help the family of today meet the challenges of change?

We believe that the clearest new direction for home economics is to help people identify and develop certain fundamental competences that will be effective in personal and family living regardless of the particular circumstances of the individual or family.

Fundamental to Effective Living are the Competences to:

- establish values which give meaning to personal, family, and community living; select goals appropriate to these values

- create a home and community environment conducive to the healthy growth and development of all members of the family at all stages of the family cycle

- achieve good interpersonal relationships within the home and within the community

- nurture the young and foster their physical, mental, and social growth and development

- make and carry out intelligent decisions regarding the use of personal, family, and community resources

- establish long-range goals for financial security and work toward their achievement

- plan consumption of goods and services—including food, clothing, and housing—in ways that will promote values and goals established by the family

- purchase consumer goods and services appropriate to an overall consumption plan and wise use of economic resources

- perform the tasks of maintaining a home in such a way that they will contribute effectively to furthering individual and family goals

- enrich personal and family life through the arts and humanities and through refreshing and creative use of leisure

- take an intelligent part in legislative and other social action programs which directly affect the welfare of individuals and families

- develop mutual understanding and appreciation of differing cultures and ways of life, and co-operate with people of other cultures who are striving to raise levels of living

As home economists, we can measure the success of our work by the extent to which we contribute to the development by individuals and families of these competences.

Challenges . . . Present and Future

What must we do if our profession is truly to "free the spirit for the more important and permanent interests of the home and of society"? How can we help individuals and families achieve satisfaction and beauty in their own lives, dignity and assurance in their relationships with others, build strength within the home and democracy in the community? How can we most effectively prepare the professional home economist for increased leadership in helping families achieve better lives?

If home economics is to meet the challenges of today and of the future, we believe it must

- serve more individuals and families and serve them more effectively
- expand research and focus it on needs of individuals and families
- strengthen education for the profession

Specific responsibilities, objectives, and programs of action for serving more people, expanding research, and strengthening education will differ with each group within the profession. All are challenged, however, to find new directions in meeting our common objectives.

CHALLENGE: To serve more individuals and families and serve them more effectively

Home economics educators are challenged to focus instruction on development of the competences important to the pattern of effective living; to co-operate in developing an educational program that will reach men, women, boys and girls of varying abilities and from different cultural, social, and economic groups; to plan for an effective progression of home economics education from one educational level to another; to increase the public understanding of home economics; and to extend home economics to other countries.

To serve more families more effectively, *home economists in business* must find more and better ways to interpret to producers and distributors the needs of families and ways of meeting them; the trends in consumers' wants and ways of living; the characteristics of products important for consumer satisfaction; and consumption patterns of families at different income levels. Through consumer education programs, home economists can increase the ability of the public to co-operate with retailers, to communicate their reaction to goods on the market, and to suggest ways in which such goods can be made more acceptable.

Home economists in institution administration and dietetics should take note of changes in family living patterns and provide services that will be most effective in performing functions increasingly taken over by agencies outside the home. Even within the past decade we have seen that more people

70

eat one or more of their three meals a day in restaurants and hotels, more young people attend college and live in college dormitories, more people enter the labor force and eat in industrial dining rooms and cafeterias, and more people take advantage of hospital and clinic care, day-care centers for children, and homes for the aged. There is renewed emphasis on the value of the school lunch program.

Home economists in social agencies should further the community's awareness of the value of the services of public and private welfare agencies and help provide knowledge and assistance that will create or improve these services. The welfare of the family is interwoven with community, national, and international conditions. Home economists can help families recognize these relationships and stimulate programs needed for better family living.

CHALLENGE: To expand research and focus it on the needs of individuals and families

Home economics must foster a vigorous research program focused on the home and on the family. Furthermore, it must increase the usefulness of research findings by making them more readily available to the profession and the public.

In planning new directions for research, home economics should place high priority on research significant to better family living in an age of rapid change. While continuing to search out new knowledge in established areas, such as nutrition, housing, and textiles, it should extend research related to the economic and managerial problems of the home and to the mental, emotional, and social aspects of family living—all of which grow in importance in an age of rapid change.

Home economics must have research workers with a breadth and depth of training which will enable them to use the tools and methods of the basic sciences. Since interdisciplinary co-operative research is increasingly used and needed to solve many problems of family living, home economists must be able to take their places as members of a team of specialists.

CHALLENGE: To strengthen education for the profession

In meeting the challenge of better education for its professional workers, home economics must establish clear objectives, re-evaluate them continuously, and set new directions in the light of:

- those individual and family competences to which the profession can contribute
- the nature of the social and scientific forces which currently influence day to day living
- the philosophy and trends of basic education with which professional education in home economics must be co-ordinated

- developments in its own and other fields of study which provide new bases for helping families.

Colleges and universities should strengthen the undergraduate curriculum in the root sciences and arts. Their programs should provide opportunity for the *depth* of education needed for leadership in particular aspects of the home economics profession and the *breadth* of education needed by those who assume leadership in civic and community affairs related to family welfare.

All professional home economics education should endeavor to develop those qualities that characterize the successful home economist. Important among these are:

- genuine concern for the family as a basic unit in society

- creativeness in extending, in applying, or in disseminating knowledge to improve personal and family living

- capacity to distinguish in the new between that which is significant and that which lacks true value for better living

- an appreciation of the lasting satisfactions to be gained from home economics as a profession

- concern with local, national, and international programs that affect family welfare.

Within its First Fifty Years
Home Economics Has . . .

- developed a unique educational program for those concerned with the home and family and especially adapted to the particular interests and responsibilities of women

- fostered and advanced the movement for preschool education; cooperated in establishing centers for child study and parent education

- conducted studies in family relations and child development which have strengthened education programs for family living throughout the country, have led to better group care of children outside the home

- built a body of literature for both professional and lay groups

- participated in initiating and sponsoring pioneer radio and television programs for homemakers

- contributed to the hygienic standards for households and institutions through continued research and teaching in household sanitation

- initiated studies of food composition and nutrition which led home economists out of "the chaos of cults and fads" and opened up a whole field of research and teaching

- provided studies of food consumption and appraisals of the nutritive value of diets which indicated common inadequacies of diets

- conducted large-scale studies of family expenditures, consumption, and savings, thereby providing data essential for programs of education and of public assistance

- contributed research findings as a basis for government policy in the public interest—for example, enrichment of bread, flour, cereals, and other food products

- supported legislation which culminated in the passage of the Food, Drug and Cosmetic Act of 1938 and subsequent amendments, and other legislation in areas of consumer protection in such federal regulatory agencies as the Federal Trade Commission

- supported legislation for the National School Lunch Act, which has brought more nutritious diets to the nation's children and far-reaching education in improved food habits

- improved the health of millions of men, women, and children through research studies in food and nutrition, through interpreting such research findings, and through teaching their application to daily diets

- developed housing plans that efficiently accommodate the activities of special groups of families, various family members, or meet the special needs of individuals

- developed methods of household management which help the homemaker make wise use of time, energy, money, and other family resources

- supplied industry with research findings which have contributed to the design and manufacture of more efficient household equipment, to the processing of food products, and to the improvement of textile products

- pioneered in an extensive study of body measurements of thousands of women and children, thus furnishing the clothing industry with a much-needed basis for standards for sizes of garments and patterns

- pioneered in research on the relation of fiber content to the wearing qualities of textiles used for household and clothing purposes—research which helped in the development of specifications for consumers' goods and stimulated informative labeling on textile materials

- opened up opportunities for professional home economists in business, in hospitals and clinics, in social welfare and public health and other important fields of service—openings from which have come such specialized professions as that of the dietitian and home economist in business

• helped protect the well-being of the nation's families in time of war, depressions, and other disasters through aiding the government in developing and initiating programs of emergency feeding, nutrition, education, food and clothing conservation, youth training, and day-care centers for children

• contributed to the well-being of families in many other countries through co-operation with government and private agencies and foundations, religious groups, and various international organizations such as the specialized agencies of the United Nations

• aided in establishing colleges of home economics in other countries and arranged home economics training in the United States for young women from abroad; participated in international conferences abroad and arranged for an international Congress on Home Economics in the United States in 1958.

PART THREE

Impacts on New Directions
1960 - 1969

Home Economics is the field of knowledge and service primarily concerned with strengthening family life through (1) educating the individual for family living, (2) improving the services used by families, (3) conducting research to discover the changing need of individuals in families and the means of satisfying these needs, (4) furthering unity, national, world conditions favorable to family living.

Home Economics synthesizes knowledge drawn from it's own research, from the physical, biological, and social sciences and the arts and applies this knowledge to improving lives of families and of individuals.

NEW DIRECTIONS
Scott, et al - 1959

10

The Next Fifty Years in Home Economics Education Research

Ruth T. Lehman
Professor in School of Home Economics at Ohio State University

This article is part of a series on research in various areas of home economics planned for the *Journal* by the research section of the American Home Economics Association. The series will be published later in bulletin form.

The early story of research in home economics education is largely one of leadership by a few institutions and individuals. At times this has been a shifting leadership (1). At first Columbia University took the lead with a 1906 master's thesis on the topic, interestingly enough, "Early History of Domestic Science." There followed in the next few years studies on the status of teacher-training in home economics in the United States, on college courses in domestic science, and on city supervision. Columbia is credited also with the first (1918) doctoral dissertation in home economics education: Murdoch's "The Measurement of Certain Elements in Hand Sewing."

Before 1920, four other institutions were reporting research in the field. These were the University of Chicago, Colorado State Teachers College, Stanford University, and George Peabody College for Teachers. In the next two decades, almost 50 additional institutions had awarded the master's degree in home economics education. By 1937 the doctor's degree had been conferred on 25 women by Columbia, University of Chicago, University of Minnesota, New York University, and Ohio State University.

Thus, from 1906 through 1936, almost 800 pieces of research were reported, some of them professional studies, but most of them students' theses. During those years, 54 institutions had reported one or more studies but only 10 had listed as many as 20 reports. These top 10 were responsible for more than half (56 percent) of the studies; Iowa State College (now University) and Columbia, for one-third (34 percent). Then followed in order, Chicago, George

76

Peabody, University of Southern California, Minnesota, Ohio State, University of Tennessee, and what were then known as Colorado A. and M. and Kansas A. and M. Colleges (now State Universities). In spite of all this activity, however, fewer than 100 reports were published, other than in books of abstracts put out by the institutions concerned.

A scanning of the research titles on curriculum alone in the late 1920's and '30's reveals certain trends in emphasis at that time (2) (3). Curriculum studies were concerned largely with the secondary school. Examination of textbooks, periodicals, or course outlines and the use of a questionnaire were the most common methods of research. The topics receiving most emphasis were aims and objectives, courses of study, and pupil activities, or interests, or problems. What a spate of activity studies we had! There was a limited amount of research on home economics for boys and on evaluation. Clothing and textiles, foods, family and social relationships, and child development were the subject areas most often involved.

Some Current Trends

In the 1930's, several things happened which do much to explain the impetus given to research from that time to the present. Beulah I. Coon was appointed in 1930 as the first research specialist in home economics education in the U. S. Office of Education. Through the years, she has given consultant service in research to colleges, states, and individuals. She has probably influenced more graduate students in our field than has any other one person. Miss Coon has worked also with the research committee of the American Vocational Association and with the research section of the American Home Economics Association. She has held conferences on graduate work in home economics education for institutions within a state and for representatives of several states. She has been responsible for research sessions at regional and national meetings, co-ordinated several co-operative research projects, and written much.

Another event was Clara Brown's appraisal of research in home economics education at the 1937 convention of the American Home Economics Association (4). She emphasized the need for more research in evaluation and strongly urged that more faculty participate in professional research. By her example in both these respects, she has done much to advance the field.

A third stimulating influence was the passage of the George-Dean Act in 1937. This Act provided vocational funds for the support of research, the first time that employment of personnel for the express purpose of research in education had been subsidized. This at last put home economics education research more nearly on the same basis as home economics subject-matter areas which had long been sponsored by Experiment Station funds.

And what are the trends? There has, first of all, been a great increase in the amount of research. In the past five years alone (1953-1958), a total of 477 master's and 84 doctoral theses were reported (5). Home economics education was second only to nutrition and foods in each of these categories. (Almost twice as many master's degrees—896, in fact—were, however, conferred without thesis; a most disquieting trend to some workers in the field.) By far the greatest number of studies were in curriculum or program planning (216 or 39 percent) and evaluation (131 or 23 percent). There was increasing emphasis on studies of college and adult programs.

As might be expected, there are now more persons engaged professionally in research. In 1937, there were four such persons; in 1959 state supervisors listed 28. Eighteen universities and at least two state departments of vocational education report that some professional research is going on (6).

There is a trend, also, toward co-operative research. The first such study on a national scale was that sponsored by the home economics section of the American Vocational Association and reported in 1948 (7). It dealt with "Factors Affecting the Satisfactions of Home Economics Teachers" and was a particularly timely study because of the teacher shortage in the schools. The study was under the chairmanship of Druzilla Kent, with a representative from each of the four regions, and with Beulah Coon as active consultant. It had the financial support of the AVA and help from various divisions of the U. S. Office of Education. State departments of vocational education in 46 states, many teaching-training institutions, and about 5,000 teachers participated.

The next co-operative study, carried by six states of the central region— Illinois, Iowa, Michigan, Minnesota, Missouri, and Ohio—is still in progress. Started in 1953, it has been concerned with certain characteristics of home economics teachers and of students preparing to be teachers; specifically, attitudes toward children, vocational interests, and attitudes toward families unlike one's own. As an outgrowth, other persons are considering a new project or group of projects.

Still another trend is toward somewhat more frequent publication. There is now a definitive statement of the scope of our research field, including illustrations of significant studies which have been made and proposals for co-operative research. This statement was prepared by Hester Chadderdon and a committee as a report to the home economics division of the Association of Land-Grant Colleges and State Universities (8). There have been more articles published. There is an occasional longer research report, such as Clara Brown Arny's book on her five-year study of 20 schools in Minnesota (9). The study now under way in the U. S. Office of Education, which will compare high school home economics offerings with those reported 20 years ago (10), may point to new directions for home economics.

As for summaries of significant research, this was for some years done in three-year cycles in the *Review of Educational Research* (11); but at present home economics studies appear there only incidentally if at all and under such general titles as administration, evaluation, and the like. A recent and first attempt of a home economics agency to provide such a summary is that of the U. S. Office of Education in inviting Ivol Spafford to review research in home economics education for 1955-56. The report—a valuable one—is in two parts; one deals with selected studies in home economics in higher education, and the other with secondary school and adult programs (12).

And What of Tomorrow?

But we look at the efforts and accomplishments of the past 50 years, or even the past 10 years, primarily that we may be better able to build in the future. And in building we must dare to be different, as were the pioneers in home economics.

Research is, in its simplest terms, "the finding of answers to problems." The record shows that we have been conferring many degrees, particularly at the master's level. Because our research has been too largely in unrelated fragments, however, we have not been getting enough meaningful answers, enough significant research. If related in topic, many studies have been too far apart in time, or too different in techniques used, or unplanned in terms of sampling to make possible a composite of results.

Perhaps the way out of our dilemma was suggested more than 20 years ago by Lydia J. Roberts as she considered the status of research throughout the field of home economics. She claimed that we begin at the wrong end in planning research. She proposed, therefore, that we first block out the major problems in the field, then break one of these down into a succession of smaller problems much as a tree is made up of smaller branches and twigs. We should study first one twig and then another until we some day reach the larger branch. "An attack of this sort," she said, "is much more significant—to continue my simile—than to be constantly on the jump from twig to twig on different trees." (13)

This suggests that even master's theses might attack significant twigs; that research at the master's level—as well as the doctoral—should make a contribution to the field.

It seems, therefore, an appropriate time to propose a new type of master's thesis; that master's students shall in effect do co-operative research. To illustrate with a simple problem: one high school teacher recently was concerned about the type of student who takes home economics as compared with those who do not elect it. She found the answers for her county. But a group of four master's students could have attacked the problem in a larger way in terms of state, or region, or the United States. They would have developed the questionnaire together and carried out a sound sampling plan. Assembling and interpreting the findings on one or perhaps two significant questions of the study and writing a report on that part would have been an individual matter. The reports together would have given us the answer; the students would have a better concept of research and a realization that they were making a contribution to their field. Group guidance on theses would have been a time-saving and rewarding technique on the part of the adviser.

A second proposal is that we honestly reconsider our now well-entrenched practice of granting the master's degree without thesis. The argument that only those who are going to be research workers should write a thesis is a debatable one. Particularly is this so if one believes that "research is a method of thinking," and that to be able to assume responsibility for the process in its entirety is a mark of intellectual development to be expected in a graduate student, and thus an important goal of a graduate program. We need seriously to consider also the advantages of a fifth-year certificate for those who wish to acquire more knowledge—in itself a most worthy aim—but who are not interested in taking, or who are unable to take, the next step toward graduate maturity.

A third proposal is that, in two or three institutions having strong graduate and research programs, we establish special training centers for the development of research leaders. Each year institutions and state departments of education come seeking workers to give part or full time to research in home economics education. This is most encouraging for progress in our field. Yet, as a rule, there are few persons if any to recommend; usually each one in her doctoral program has had only the experience of her dissertation as preparation. If such centers would each carry on several programs of research and make it possible for qualified students to register for credit in research procedures, we might well have the answer. This would make it possible for interested graduate students from different colleges to go for a time to one of the centers for first-hand experience with a variety of the more common types of studies in our field. The center should have available pertinent courses in research methods and statistics. It should provide for enough of both that the student has some facility and confidence in their use.

Another proposal is that we do more in the way of important co-operative research, both within an institution and among a group of colleges or states. And this may well come as more groups take advantage of the opportunities afforded since 1954 under Public Law 531 (14). One co-operative project in home economics education has been presented in application for funds and is now well under way.

Wherever co-operative research has been tried, the experience has been found to be a stimulating one, and real growth in research ability of the participants has resulted. However, there are certain precautions which earlier workers would pass on to others. It is important to start with a fairly small problem, which can be completed within a reasonable length of time. Not only does this limit the complexity of the procedures but it gives the workers the satisfaction of seeing their results sooner. It makes results available at once to others in the field who can begin to act on them. It is important also to consider the cost of each proposed study realistically in terms of time, personnel, and money. It is frustrating to carry a study just so far, and then discover that one lacks the facilities to complete it.

A final proposal is the old and familiar one that we make our findings more available. There should be more articles published, and more should appear in education journals. But we need more than reports of single studies. We need summaries of groups of studies. We have seen that in the past five years, there were 131 graduate theses which were classified under evaluation research. Yet, who is aware of the kind of instruments or procedures which may thereby be available for use in the classroom or in research? And who knows which of these tools are promising and worth while? Several theses could be set up to appraise these 131 reports and the findings assembled in pamphlet form.

The possibility of whether the U. S. Office of Education, after the success of its first attempt, might continue to assume the responsibility for developing summaries from time to time is worth thoughtful consideration. Or perhaps the American Home Economics Association could be the sponsor. We have all appreciated the special research issue of the *Journal* initiated several years ago. Some of us have hoped also for the day when the Association would go even further, issuing an annual volume of review in research in given home economics areas, these areas appearing in probably a three-year cycle, as is the case with the *Review of Educational Research*. There would thus be in each volume a three-year review of significant research in one or two areas; it should be of interest and value to many home economists. . . . The next 50 years sound interesting for the researcher.

References

1. Studies and Research in Home Economics Education Reported by Colleges and Universities. U. S. Office of Education Misc. 1163, Revised Feb. 1937. (Mimeographed).

2. Welch, Lila M., and Lingenfelter, Mary R. Studies of the Home Economics Curriculum: An Annotated Bibliography. Bibliographies in Education, No. 1, Bureau of Educational Research, Ohio State University, Columbus, 1930.

3. Bibliography of Studies of the Home Economics Curriculum, 1926-1934. Prepared by a Committee of the Home Economics Section of the Association of Land-Grant Colleges and Universities. U. S. Office of Education, Vocational Bull. No. 179, Home Econ. Series No. 17 (1934), [Supply exhausted].

4. Brown, C. M. Appraisal of trends in home economics education research. *J. Home Econ.* **29** (Nov. 1937), pp. 603-606.

5. Titles of Completed Theses in Home Economics and Related Fields in Colleges and Universities of the United States. Annual issues for 1953-54 to 1957-58, inclusive. Agricultural Research Service, U. S. Department of Agriculture, or Office of Education, Department of Health, Education, and Welfare.

6. Personal communication from the Home Economics Education Service, U. S. Office of Education.

7. Home Economics Research Committee. Factors Affecting the Satisfactions of Home Economics Teachers. A.V.A. Research Bull. No. 3. American Vocational Association, Washington, D. C., 1948.

8. Chadderdon, H., *et al.* Research in Home Economics Education, in *Areas of Home Economics Research, 1947 - 1956*. Reports to the Committee on Research, Division of Home Economics, Association of Land-Grant Colleges and State Universities, 1958. [Mimeographed and distributed to member institutions. Supply exhausted].

9. Arny, C. B. *The Effectiveness of the High School Program in Home Economics.* Minneapolis, Minn.: University of Minnesota Press, 1952.

10. Home Economics in Public High Schools: 1988-89. U. S. Office of Education, Voc. Div. Bull. No. 213, Home Econ. Educ. Series No. 24 (1941) [Supply exhausted].

11. *Review of Educational Research* 11, No. 4, Part 1 (Oct. 1941), pp. 387-397; **14**, No. 4 (Oct. 1944), pp. 301-310; **17**, No. 3 (June 1947), pp. 209-221; **20**, No. 4 (Oct. 1950), pp. 299-308.

12. Spafford, I., in co-operation with E. P. Amidon. Studies on the Teaching of Home Economics in Colleges and Universities, 1955-56. U. S. Office of Education, Voc. Div. Bull. No. 276, Home Econ. Series No. 31. U. S. Government Printing Office, Washington 25, D. C., 1959, 55 cents. (A similar bulletin on secondary and adult program studies will be available later.)

13. Roberts, L. J. Is home economics research meeting its challenge? *J. Home Econ.* **29** (Dec. 1937), pp. 677-682.

14. Information about the Cooperative Research Program of the Office of Education under Public Law 531 and instructions for preparing applications for support of Cooperative Research Projects. Available directly from the Cooperative Research Program, U. S. Office of Education, Washington 25, D. C.

11

The Place of Home Economics In American Society

Gordon W. Blackwell
President of Florida State University

This article is based on his address before the Home Economics Section of the Association of Southern Agricultural Workers in Jacksonville, Florida, on February 5.

The challenge of change is perhaps greater for no single body of knowledge than for home economics. This challenge is necessitated not only by the rapid technological, social, and economic developments in modern American living but also by the enormous growth of the educational institutions which offer instruction in home economics and by the expansion of their research programs and extension services. These changes must on occasion leave the home economist feeling very confused.

In such exigencies, one tends to forget his past accomplishments, and I would urge you to review now and then the accomplishments of your profession. From such perspectives as the excellent summary in "Home Economics—New Directions," you can better outline the future.

If the place of home economics in American society is to remain as vital a part as it has been in these last 50 years, it must, it seems to me, remain alert to the changes in our society—in particular, the changing role of women in our society. For her role is changing, and home economics will have to change with it. This being true, my remarks are largely devoted to some of the changes that sociologists have noted in recent studies, especially as they affect the women in our society.

Of profound significance is the steadily lowering age of marriage since World War II. Twenty is now the average age of marriage for women. Marriage has invaded not only college student bodies but our high schools as well. As aptly stated by Audrey K. Wilder, the "Pomp and Circumstance" of the commencement processional vies with the strains of Mendelssohn's Wedding March. Too frequently Mendelssohn wins out. Education takes a loss.

Looking at the other end of the life span, we know that women live longer than men by six years on the average. This means that there are more women than men in the population. Furthermore, there are economic implications for women who marry since they can expect to be widowed unless the marriage is broken for other reasons, as is more and more often the case.

It is clear also that an increasing proportion of our citizens will be in the older age brackets in the future. From 3 percent over 65 years of age in 1850, the proportion increased to 9 percent in 1960, with the prediction of almost 13 percent by 1975. The psychological, social, and leisure needs of aging persons, *most of whom will be women,* present a challenge to the home economist.

The population of the United States has always been characterized by high mobility. In our history we have already seen the long-continuing westward movement, the great streams of immigrants from Europe, and the continual farm to city movement. Since 1920 many millions more people have left farms and gone to urban places than have migrated to farms. The majority of these cityward migrants have been women.

It is as though a giant egg beater has been at work in the nation's population. Families and single individuals have been spewed in all directions, with the main streams being from country to city, from South to North, and from East to Far West.

In addition to this relatively long-range migration, people have been quite mobile within their community of residence. Truly a high proportion of the American people are not anchored to hearth and home. And this high mobility can be expected to continue for some time. Young people, especially girls, must be prepared for high mobility of residence.

The growth of cities is reflected in changes in the occupational structure. In 1820, some 62 percent of the labor force were agricultural workers; in 1960 it was approximately 8 percent. This decline may be expected to continue slowly during the next several decades as agriculture becomes further mechanized and as more and more people enter industry, business, the professions, technical jobs, and service occupations. The proportion of workers who are in the professions has steadily increased as the American economy has become mature, and this trend will continue for some time yet.

Along with industrialization have come increasingly frequent opportunities for women in the world of work. In 1890 less than a fifth of American women were in the labor force at any given time; today the proportion is more than a third, with women earning $42 billion yearly in salaries and wages. Three out of every ten married women are working, and two out of every five mothers whose youngest child is of school age are in the labor force. Today the average age of a mother when the youngest child reaches six years is 32.

The more education a woman has, the more apt she is to be working. About half who are college graduates are working or seeking work at any given time. College girls today will work not three or five years but, some say, an average of more nearly 25 years—a prospect which most of our college students are currently not willing to accept.

There are many reasons which lead women to work in increasing numbers. Homemaking no longer need involve endless hours of manual labor as in former times. Furthermore, many women become dissatisfied with the chit-chat of afternoon bridge parties or with listening to the perennial minutes being read in a so-called study club. They desire to feel productive. Many want to keep intellectually alive and consequently move into one of the professions. Many families find it difficult to make ends meet in the face of the high cost of living, and, therefore, the wife works as soon as the youngest child reaches school age.

There is every indication that these trends relative to women and work will continue in the future and, in fact, may accelerate.

Effects on Women

And now for a look at personality development. The individual in any society faces the necessity of charting his own course of development somewhere between putty-like conformity to prescribed cultural norms and legal prescriptions on the one hand and autonomous personal action on the other.

In American society, the pressure for conformity by women is great, varying from region to region, from community to community, and among different social strata and groups. Although these pressures are certainly real, we have a culture and social structure in considerable ferment and change. The many new social patterns provide a maze of multiple statuses and roles for each woman and often involve frustrating conflict. Her probable mobility adds to the complexities facing her. Changing values in the society make it difficult for her to keep her social moorings. The culture and social structure often do not provide her with sufficiently clear guidelines and high predictability in interpersonal relations. The social situation sometimes is not clearly defined for her. Social adjustment too frequently proves difficult. According to a noted sociologist, Robin Williams, "If such disillusion of the social pattern involves values central to the person's self-identity, the shattering of stable social expectations seems catastrophic for personality integration." It is not surprising, then, that psychiatrists bear witness to the high incidence of mental breakdowns among women.

Women are faced with a complexity of roles to play and frequently find themselves on shifting sand. There are indications that these problems of maintaining a stable personality at various points in the life cycle are more difficult to cope with for women than for men. For one thing, the stereotypic dependent feminine role comes into apparent conflict with intellectual role models and with concepts of independence and quality. These problems are of considerable concern to those engaged in working with girls and young women.

Global Outlook

Finally, global trends of the first half of the twentieth century dictate that we cannot confine ourselves to preparing the individual for life in a local community or for narrow nationalism. We must seek to develop a sense of responsibility that is no less than global, one which stretches even to the outer reaches of the universe. International shifts in power, technological developments in transportation, communication, and war making, as well as the spread of education among the masses of the world, have resulted in bringing international problems to our very doorstep as the oceans have become as mere lakes and as man probes into outer space. Women in tomorrow's world must be motivated to develop sympathetic understanding of complex foreign affairs.

In the past 50 to 100 years, women in America have achieved a large measure of equality of opportunity with men—equality in the ballot, in many occupations, in family life, and in most other important matters. Women now cast approximately as many ballots as men in the national elections, outnumber men as stockholders in America's great corporations, control at least 60—some say as high as 85—percent of all personal expenditures.

Progress has been made also toward equality in education. For example, in 1890 fewer than 3,000 women graduated annually from American colleges and universities. Seventy years later the number is over 135,000, and it appears certain that women will obtain a college education with increasing frequency in the future.

And yet we know that many competent girls who graduate from high school with a high academic record do not enter college. Too often the girl or her parents do not see the values in a college education for her. If there is a brother, he will usually get first chance at the financial resources of the family. Whereas more than half of the graduates from our secondary schools are women, only a third of the college enrollment are women.

Based on ability tests, a study by the National Science Foundation of those in the top quarter of high school graduates who do not go on to college estimated the number at between 100,000 and 200,000 annually. Girls account for an alarming proportion of this loss of talented human resources. This "feminine fallout," to borrow a felicitous phrase from the *Wall Street Journal,* may be as serious as the threat of atomic fallout.

Kind of Preparation

This brings us then to the question of what kind of preparation is needed for women of tomorrow's world. And what will be the place of home economics in their education? What should be the pattern of extension services and of research? Whatever the specific answers, the home economist will have the continuous task of adapting to the realities of a rapidly changing society. Home economics will have to take into account a society in which there will be many more aged persons, especially women. It will have to take into account the trend toward early marriages, rapid mobility, continuing urbanization, and higher proportions of women in business, technical jobs, and the professions. Above all, it must prepare women for a society in which frustrations and role conflicts, resulting from these changes, will be the rule rather than the exception. Indeed, I venture to say that the place of home economics in American society will be directly determined by the extent to which its services, its curriculums, and its research programs are tailored to fit these realities.

I share with you a concern that home economics should take steps to adjust effectively to these changes. Although I realize that the number of earned degrees in home economics has not kept pace with the total enrollment of women in our colleges during the past decade, I am not among those who believe that home economics is sick. I know that your emphases in home economics education in the secondary schools, in college-level curriculums, in graduate programs, in research, and in extension services have been changing, particularly within the past 15 years. I believe the decreasing emphasis upon skills and the increasing attention to application of the social and natural sciences to problems relating to homemaking are illustrative of desirable changes.

"Yes, but what more can we do?" you ask. To this question, I'm afraid I see no easy answers. I am not trained in your discipline, and it would be presumptuous of me to make specific proposals even if I did imagine that I could be of help. As an outsider, however, particularly as a university president, I would propose certain general lines of endeavor.

First, as I've indicated earlier, you can make a rigorous effort to re-evaluate course offerings in the light of modern American society. How essential is the skill or the subject matter of this or that course to a woman as she actually lives her life today, not as she used to live it and not as she ought to live it— but as she does live it? In this connection, a continuation of the lessening of emphasis upon skills seems to be in order in educational programs, especially at the secondary school level. There is much evidence that the better students are not being sufficiently challenged by intellectual content of some of the courses. I need not remind you, I am sure, that no longer is it fashionable for a young woman to bank the fire of her brain.

Second, I suggest provisions in the college curriculum which would require home economics undergraduate and graduate students to go outside their department or school for a sound foundation in chemistry and biology, or in psychology and sociology, or in general economics. It is perhaps a truism to say that, as an applied discipline, home economics must have mastery of the fundamentals which are to be applied. After all, are not the really significant contributions in applied fields such as food and nutrition or clothing and textiles to be found in a thorough grounding in chemistry and biology? Do not the main avenues to new insights in child development, family living, and household management derive from psychology, sociology, and economics? Again I say that skills are less important in these kinds of activities than are basic scientific knowledge and decision-making ability regarding the management of family resources. And, as home economics comes to stress these matters universally—not just in the best universities—more men will be attracted into the field.

Third, I urge increased emphasis upon research and creative activity on the part of home economists. Most of this will take place either in the universities or in industry, sometimes on a co-operative basis between the two. If my previous suggestions are valid, then the requirement of greatly expanded research programs becomes clear, and the necessary dependence of home economics research upon the tools and concepts of the natural and social sciences need not be argued further.

Next, I would stress the obligation of schools of home economics and extension services to provide professional opportunities for women who, at age 30 to 40, find their youngest child in school and wish to engage in worthwhile work. Some of these have previous training in home economics and merely need retreading for a summer or two. Others will want to earn a master's degree in the process of job preparation. Still others will need to complete an undergraduate degree. Among hundreds of thousands of women such as these each year, there is a vast reservoir of potential professional womanpower which you must tap effectively with planned programs. In this endeavor, both the colleges and the extension services should be prepared to serve as educational and vocational counseling centers for these women who symbolize in their numbers and purpose a relatively new feature of American society.

Finally, I believe some serious thinking about the basic purposes of home economics is in order. From such thinking could emerge a modified concept of what home economics is and what it has to offer the modern homemaker. Conceivably, a fresh concept—perhaps even a new name—broadened to include more of the liberal arts and sciences, together with more concern for the attitudes, values, and decision-making ability of the homemaker than with skills, would open new and broader avenues of service. This emphasis on general culture, intellectual development, and the multiple possibilities of a strong undergirding in the natural and social sciences together with the traditional concern for the ways and means to the best in family living which has always characterized home economics, could lead to an even more significant place for home economics in American society.

12

Is Salomon's House
a Modern Utopia?

Icie Macy Hoobler
Consultant to the Merrill-Palmer Institute in Detroit

This article is adapted from Dr. Hoobler's talk at the meeting of the research section during the 1962 annual meeting of the American Home Economics Association in Miami Beach in June.

The debt the modern world owes to science is so pervasive and so profound that no man can measure it. But before science and its resultant technologies could be freed for their development in the modern world, a revolution in human attitudes had to be achieved, and that revolution was not accomplished solely by the continuous impact of scientific discovery. Men's minds had to be prepared, older habits of thought challenged, and the areas of faith enlarged. The idea and the ideals of science had to be brought home to the human heart and mind. The idea and the ideals found their architect and their spokesman in Francis Bacon . . . incomparably the greatest poet of science. The core of his thought is the dignity of man and the greatness of man's future. His ultimate vision reaches far beyond our own times to embrace the conception of a unified science spanning the whole realm of the knowable, by which man's command of himself and of nature may be joined.—From the Introduction by Hugh G. Dick to *Selected Writings of Francis Bacon*. (1)

Today, when all too often we feel ourselves being swept helplessly on by the great torrent of science, there is solace as well as strength in historical perspective. There is also inspiration in the knowledge that the great ideas of mankind grow and continue century after century as the above quotation suggests.

In 1961, we celebrated the 400th anniversary of the birth of Sir Francis Bacon, the prophet of the forthcoming scientific and technical age. Although not a scientist, he wanted to help scientists fulfill their social responsibilities.

I believe that his fable of the *New Atlantis* carries a message for the home economist and the American Home Economics Association although they did not come into being until this century. You will recall that the New Atlantis was depicted as a utopian society guided by scholars who devoted themselves to scientific research, to organization of knowledge, and the pursuit of wisdom. In Salomon's House, the symbol of this society, Bacon depicted his ideal of a scientific way of life. Salomon's House was truly an organized scientific laboratory ruled intelligently by scientific philosophers. All the research work, done by teams (if you will) of scientists co-operating together, was aimed directly to benefit mankind. Salomon's House was the most useful and highly respected of all the institutions in the utopian society of the New Atlantis. Indeed, it was the lantern of the Kingdom.

To me, Salomon's House seems prophetic of a home economics research laboratory.

For me, much of home economics research can be traced to the social influence of Sir Francis Bacon. His fictitious workers were organized in separate sections and divisions, and they conducted research in many fields. Studies were directed toward how to maintain health and cure disease; to foods; to fabrics; to dyes; to radiation. Other divisions were concerned with investigations on telescopes and microscopes; on engines; on sound, on controlling its quality, transmitting it over long distances; on airplanes; and on submarines.

Bacon's utopian research, based on scientific progress through scientific co-operation, had wise men who believed in applying knowledge for the good of mankind. They were organized into groups, each with a special function, according to the principle of division of labor. All laboratory data were available to all. As in today's team research, some scientists planned the work, others were *doers* of experiments, while still others recorded organized information of fundamental importance to the people of New Atlantis. Finally, there were three "that raise the former discoveries by experiments into greater observations, axioms and aphorisms. These we call *Interpreters of Nature*." We might well question whether Salomon's House by today's standards and needs would be a utopia. However, Bacon's imprint has been made on a scientific society that is now emerging after 400 years. I urge each of you to reread the *New Atlantis*.

Most of us have been literally swallowed up with the coming of the space age, with its vast opportunities and responsibilities, vast technological advances, vast areas of new knowledge and the great power generated through the precepts, principles, and accomplishments often associated with the fabled Salomon's House.

Bacon conceived of scientific knowledge as only for the *benefit of mankind and not for the pleasure of the mind.* In our present decade, however, we have learned that the application of scientific knowledge may be used for the good of all mankind, though unfortunately it may also be used for evil and sinister purposes. Science and technology have not yet created a perfect society. Utopia is still the challenge to mankind.

Let us consider our part in this continued striving for a perfect society from the point of view of the scientists that we in home economics are sending forth to contribute to this effort. What can we say today of home economics research as a training ground for scholarship, leadership, and individual fulfillment?

Home economics research is a natural beachhead for enlarging the concept and dimensions of Salomon's House. Productive scientists approach problems in all sorts of ways and by different methods (both rational and empirical) and attitudes. There are secrets in every phase of the game. Just as Sir Francis Bacon blew the clarion call which wakened the world to the fact that science could transform society so there are latent opportunities for stimulating young people to greater intellectual heights and greater personal satisfactions that are sometimes missed among the *doings* and the troubles encountered in research. The leaders of Salomon's House emphasized the concept of continued scientific progress through scientific co-operation. If we work from the vantage point of designing and building into that design opportunity in the research process to enhance scholarship, provide opportunity for leadership, and a sense of personal worth and accomplishment, the ranks of science will close in with those who have the aptitude and are qualified to think creatively and constructively and to act enthusiastically. Scientists, like all people, are capable of reaching greater heights through encouragement and personal appreciation at whatever level.

The world needs curious, receptive, and creative scholars versed in the knowledge and skills of home economics as well as in other areas of learning. Home economics research, whether it is designed as solo or ensemble variety, if thoughtfully conceived amid the magnificent and abundant opportunities that are at our doorstep, can become a beachhead for launching thinking, creative, and productive persons into a world that needs their contributions and services. There is a richness of experience in research and searching for truth and new knowledge that transcends other satisfactions. The home economist as well as other investigators can design studies in such a way that the objectives of the plan are attained, and at the same time a very rich dividend can be added—*that of preparing and stimulating receptive minds to greater attainment and personal satisfaction.* These are not the products of specialization but rather stimulation. Students must be encouraged to take advantage of greater opportunities, and there must be basic incentives for them.

Enlargement of Goals

It is my belief that home economists are in an admirable position to enlarge their goals in research by (1) taking a more aggressive role through interdisciplinary study of child and family life and (2) raising sights by providing more basic incentives to persons participating in organized research. Organized scientific research can be conceived and projected with triple purpose, that of obtaining the basic facts for which the investigation poses the need, enlarging knowledge and experience of the workers, and rewarding the worker by a well-rounded research experience. This last includes active participation in every phase from designing the investigation, experiencing some of the trouble and disappointments that arise in setting up the investigation, marshalling of all the interdisciplinary forces into collecting accurate data, assembling the data for interpretation, and having a real part in presentation of the results for publication. Until a scientist has had all of these experiences he has been short-changed in a research experience and in the individual fulfillment that research can provide. Organized research conceived on a wider scope of experience can contribute new woof and warp that will strengthen the fabric of scientific society—and it is here to stay. A research laboratory is an educational institution—it is an institution for education of the research worker. More consideration should be given to this phase. Laboratory experimentation is an educational process of the highest order.

If a research project is to be successful, it must be undertaken with the determination of capitalizing on the excellence of the contribution of each member of the team, give and encourage creative thinking, and establish an atmosphere of respect, faith, and acceptance of the fact that all are learning together. No scientific team can solve its internal conflicts unless its members are lifted above the tensions of the moment by powerful shared purposes. Nor, might I add, can any other team.

Varieties of Excellence

In the organized research laboratory, there are different varieties of excellence, each contributing to the success of the work done. There is the kind of intellectual activity that leads to a new theory and the kind that leads to new techniques or instruments. There is the mind that works best in quantitative terms and the mind that luxuriates in human relations. The skill of the dishwasher may find effective expression in clean glassware (without contaminations). There is excellence in record making, in typing reports. Indeed research demands excellence in craftsmanship, in technical work, in leadership, and in human relations.

Gardner in *Excellence* (2) emphasizes that in organized work greatness cannot be attained unless individuals at many levels of ability accept the need for high standards of performance and strive to achieve those standards within the limits possible for them. Success depends on universal striving for good performance.

The slogan of a research laboratory should be "Come and Learn with Me." This means I accept you as a partner and believe in you. Involvement, experience, and basic incentives are necessary for growth. Some persons are fearful of themselves and this stamps out creativity. The important thing in this changing world is *willingness to become mature—and to grow toward maturity* in thoughts and actions, not necessarily only in knowing. I am glad to see a growing recognition that home economics must make changes to better prepare students and staff for emergence into the atomic age and a scientific civilization. I believe we are recognizing that watered down courses or the removal from the home economics curriculum of fundamental courses in science and the humanities will not intellectually fortify an individual to live in a scientific society, much less make a positive contribution to it. We must be aware that science and technology are the most powerful forces unleashed by man. The changes these forces bring—and will continue to bring—run wide and deep through our society. Physical, mental, and spiritual well-being may be affected by them. Although we may not be friendly to them, they are here to be reckoned with. We must be aware of both their good and evil uses to act wisely.

Our Professional Association

The American Home Economics Association has become a federation of interests and specialties. Is the proliferation in number simply the exercise of the American habit of organizing? Are we focusing sufficiently on inter-disciplinary matters to as great extent as is possible? What is the image of home economics to be in the atomic age? These are problems that all scientific societies are faced with. Alden H. Emery, executive secretary of the American Chemical Society, in a talk before the National Research Council last April concerning the role of scientific and technical societies in modern scientific civilization, said this about services to be rendered:

> While it is the individual scientist who alone or as a member of a team is responsible for extending our knowledge of scientific fact and theory and for translating it into useful products, organized science plays a vital role.
>
> The educator role of scientific societies goes further than this. The improvement of the qualifications and real productivity of their members is inherent in the aims of most.
>
> The activities of scientific societies should contribute more than "tools" and "intellectual inspiration" to their members. They should attempt to encourage the development of an environment conducive to maximum scientific achievement. A Society must help the scientist find and fulfill his proper role in a civilization increasingly influenced and even dominated by science and technology. (3)

There was never a time in history when there were so many thrilling things to be done and changes to be wrought. The great game of life is to take advantage of every opportunity possible to serve mankind. I have learned that personal satisfactions are enriched by working and learning with others. Indeed involvement and experiences of many kinds and enterprises benefiting others have been essential for growth in mind and spirit. They mature the character and build courage to suppress fears. There have been years of searching for new knowledge through research, teaching, and facing realities of a professional career.

To those in home economics research and to those who will come to it in the future, then, I would say:

1. Take advantage of opportunities for creativity, leadership, scholarship, and basic incentives that are available for self-fulfillment and personal satisfaction.

2. Recognize and respect different varieties of excellence in craftsmanship, in technical work, in leadership, and in human relations.

3. Seek humility and perpetual self-discovery and change to realize one's best self.

4. Acquire interest in people and seek to enlarge one's goals and experiences through learning with others.

5. Acquire the love of work and service—we are all serving someone.

6. Suppress boredom and wastage of human talents through giving of one's self for the benefit of others.

7. Resolve internal conflicts through powerful shared purposes, good performance, progress, and co-operation in an atmosphere of learning together.

Let us all set our sights of service and performance high that tomorrow's scientific society may enjoy the fruits of peace and a full measure of physical, mental, and spiritual well-being.

Let us not build fears and displeasures that the scientific age is to be reckoned with. As Robert A. Millikan, the great physicist, said, "Science is after all merely the growth of man's understanding of his world, and hence his ability to live wisely in it."

References

1. *Selected Writings of Francis Bacon.* New York: The Modern Library, 1955, pp. ix, x, 543-584.

2. Gardner, J. W. *Excellence. Can We Be Equal and Excellent, Too?* New York: Harper and Brothers, Publishers, 1961.

3. Emery, A. H. The Role of Scientific and Technical Societies. *News Report, National Academy of Sciences-National Research Council* 12, No. 2 (Mar.-Apr., 1962), p. 21.

13

Values In
Home Economics

Marjorie M. Brown
Professor of Home Economics Education

The goals of a field of professional study are more adequately accomplished when they are clearly defined. In this analytical article, the author deals briefly with how values *could* enter home economics and more fully with where values *do* enter the foundations of the field, and argues that there is a new necessity for home economists to acquire rational knowledge and seek some agreement about the core of common values in home economics.

When we speak of values in home economics we could speak of three different ways in which values enter home economics. First, we could speak of values as the object of scientific study. Here we would be concerned with research and its results as subject matter about values. This subject matter would contain definitions of such terms as "absolute values," generalizations such as "consistent unilateral training in childhood results in a person's holding absolute values," and theories such as one which would explain through a set of generalizations how or why it is that consistent unilateral training does result in a person's developing absolute values.

A second and different way of referring to values in home economics would be to speak of values as statements or postulates of truth in the subject matter of home economics. In this interpretation we would consider whether the subject matter of home economics contains such statements as: "It is wrong to teach a child to hold absolute values," "A family should budget its income," "Large pieces of furniture should not be placed diagonally across the corners of a room," or "An adult should drink a pint of milk daily." Many home economists object to having values enter into home economics subject matter in this way, but it is a practice which some follow.

A third meaning when we speak of values in home economics is to refer to what is considered desirable by home economists in the pursuit of home economics as a field of study and a profession. Here the concern is for what home economists should try to accomplish *as home economists* and for ways of thinking and acting which should characterize home economists in their work. While the first two meanings of values in home economics would be interesting and worthy of exploration, the statement here is limited to the third, which will be recognized as fundamental or basic to the other two.

In this discussion of the values in home economics as a field of professional study, an attempt will be made to do the following three things and in this order:

1. Examine a definition of "value" so that the context in which values in home economics are looked at will, it is hoped, carry the meaning intended
2. Explore the points at which values enter the structure of home economics (as they enter any professional field), illustrating with some of the values made explicit when home economics was admitted to colleges and universities
3. Recognize the significance of openly identifying our values in home economics and of working toward rational agreement concerning certain of our values

A Definition of "Value"

There are many definitions of "value" and, as with many other words in the English language, the meaning differs according to the purpose and motives of the user. For our purpose in looking at values about a field of study, I will use a definition stated by the late Clyde Kluckhohn, an anthropologist: "A value is a conception, explicit or implicit, distinctive of an individual or characteristic of a group, of the desirable which influences the selection from available modes, means, and ends of action" (1, p. 395). Because the definition is influential in understanding our topic, some of the phrases need to be examined in the context in which we are thinking of values in home economics.

First, a value "influences the selection from available modes, means, and ends of action." Our conceptions of the desirable in home economics as a field serve as standards by which we *as home economists* are influenced to choose, professionally, within the limits of alternatives we see as open to us. Areas in which we are influenced in our choosing are "modes, means, and ends of action."

"Ends of action" are what we consider desirable to accomplish or to result from our action as home economists. For example, we can value producing a society in which human life and human well-being are more important than material things *or* we can value producing a society in which material things are of such importance that they are to be sought without regard to the physical

97

and mental well-being of persons who are affected by the seeking. We can value production of human personality which is sound, mature, fully functioning, creative in giving direction to the culture, *or* we can value production of persons who are unsound, immature, subservient to the culture, and sick in functioning. We can value having the work of home economists result in human group life in which the potential of all members is respected, freed, and developed *or* we can value having our work lead to human group life which is destructive of the potential of some members in order to serve the special needs and interests of others.

"Means of action" concern what we would *do* as home economists to reach some end which we value as a profession. Should we use knowledge or allow ignorance to produce the kind of society, the kind of personality, the kind of group life we value? If we use knowledge, to what should we appeal for selecting or verifying that knowledge which is "good": personal whim? the ability to shout the loudest or to carry the biggest club? the status of the speaker or writer who bestows knowledge upon us? tradition? divine revelation? the use of human intelligence in interpreting experience? "Modes of action" are the styles or ways in which an action is done or is carried out. If human intelligence is valued as a means of determining what knowledge is good, would the same mode of using human intelligence be used in producing the kind of society, kind of personality, kind of human group life valued as the mode used to predict and control inert objects of nature?

As stated in our definition, the conception of the desirable may be *explicit* or it may be *implicit*. This point is especially important as we examine values in a field of study. Values are explicit when we openly and clearly recognize them and verbalize them in undisguised terms. If, for example, a member of a college faculty in home economics speaks out against a curriculum in which students study material things *per se,* isolated from any consideration of the effect of such things upon human individuals and human society, she might say, "I realize here that I am placing value both on human welfare (as opposed to materialism) and on unity of knowledge for students in our field (as opposed to fractionization of knowledge)." On the other hand, we may make selections among available modes, means, and ends of action without being clear about the values involved in the alternatives available and in the selections we make. Under such conditions we cannot verbally state from our own knowledge the values involved, although they are *implicit* in the choices available and are potentially capable of being verbalized.

When values are not made explicit they are unrecognized and unstated assumptions about what is desirable. For example, a home economist may support the study of clothing selection taught on the basis of the students' personal or self improvement in appearance being a major outcome of such a course. Further support might be given by stating that such improvement of a student's personal appearance leads to her (or his) increased social acceptability and psychological comfort. In taking the position outlined, there are certain values assumed: (1) that education (through courses taught) should uphold hedonistic principles; (2) that all people should accept other persons on the basis of external cues, such as appearance, rather than or more than on the basis of internal cues, such as ways of thinking, ways used for need satisfaction, and so on; and (3) that people should satisfy their needs psychologically by means of outer adornment.

According to our definition, conceptions of the desirable are "distinctive of an individual or characteristic of a group." This simply says that the value concepts one person holds bear the unique interpretation or meaning which that person places on various modes, means, and ends of action. That is, to become a person's own concepts, values must be internalized; merely verbalizing about a value does not assure that the conception of the desirable has really become a part of the speaker's own thinking and distinctive of him. However, values not only characterize the thinking and action of an individual; they also delineate the character of a group. Thus, a group can be described, in terms of its values, as altruistic or materialistic or democratic; or it may be said to uphold a particular value, such as "getting along with others" or "independent thinking."

Now let us turn to how values characterize a professional group such as home economists and, thereby, the field of home economics. We are not concerned here with all values that persons who are home economists might hold—only with those values which have something to do with our selection of modes, means, and ends of action *as home economists*. We are *not* dealing here with *what* the values in home economics *ought to be* or with *where* they *ought to be* but *where, in fact,* values *do enter* the structure of home economics explicitly or implicitly. Anyone can find them if he knows what to look for; knowing where to look, makes the finding simpler.

Where Values Enter the Structure of Home Economics

Values concerning home economics as a field enter at a number of places in the over-all structure of the field. In order to make this point clear, it is necessary for us to examine this structure. Such a structure is not one somebody just makes up and says, "This is the structure of home economics;" rather it is a logical reconstruction of the thinking which goes on when one thinks and acts as a home economist. In this sense, using the word "structure" when we speak of a field of study is somewhat like its use when we speak of the structure of a sentence with its subject and predicate and its modifying words, phrases, and clauses. By logically reconstructing a sentence, we often can improve upon it because it is now more clearly open to examination. By logically reconstructing a field of study, we can see things about it which can be improved which we might not otherwise see. Here we will be looking at the structure of home economics at an over-all level and will not get involved in the structure of the parts (although this latter is important, too). At this overall level, the structure of home economics is similar to that for other so-called helping professions, such as social work, medicine, or teaching.

Let us begin at a point in the structure which is familiar to us. We are all aware that in order to be a professional home economist, one must acquire certain knowledge considered difficult or complex enough that it must be pursued at a college or university level. We are also aware that professional home economists contribute to this knowledge by addition, revision, and organization through research. Such knowledge is composed of terminology and definitions of terms, classifications, sets of data, generalizations drawn from data, and theories which organize generalizations into sets or coherent structures. Although some of this knowledge may be drawn from basic disciplines such as psychology and biology, let us call this knowledge "Home Economics Theory." (See figure 1.)

Now, any person with an inquiring mind will begin to ask questions about Home Economics Theory. For example, since home economics deals with some of the same concepts, generalizations, and theories dealt with in other fields, how is home economics differentiated from these other fields? If home economics is a profession which uses some of the knowledge produced in other fields, what are home economists trying to accomplish; that is, *as* home economists? Do home economists produce any knowledge of their own in the field, or is all of it borrowed? If home economists do produce knowledge of their own in the field, what methods of inquiry are used as the source of such knowledge? What standards and procedures for agreement are used by home economists to determine when a statement is worthy of being called "knowledge"?

These are questions which are not answered within Home Economics Theory; yet they are questions which we *do* answer, whether the answers are made explicit or whether they are only implicit in our actions as home economists. Up to this time, there is little doubt that home economists have answered these questions about home economics theory more frequently implicitly than explicitly; that is, the answers are usually unrecognized and unstated assumptions, but they are there. (The results of such unrecognized and unstated assumptions in home economics are dealt with a bit later.) These interrelated questions and their answers are outside of and more abstract than Theory, and yet they influence the focus and content of Theory. Consequently, we have two different areas of thought which can be symbolized graphically with a sign of directional influence. This set of assumptions which we make explicitly or implicitly about Home Economics Theory can be assigned any name we choose; here it will be called Meta-Theory or, if you like, Meta-Home-Economics, where the prefix "meta" is used in the sense in which sociologists refer to meta-sociology, biologists to meta-biology, and so on. (See figure 2.)

An important difference exists between home economics and the basic sciences, such as biology, psychology, and sociology, and this difference must be examined to complete the over-all structure of home economics. Mature students in the basic sciences say that their particular area of knowledge is important simply in understanding the world, in predicting events and relationships between and among phenomena. Although they may hope that the knowledge they produce and teach may benefit mankind in other ways besides the satisfaction of understanding what is around and in man himself, basic scientists are not *as scientists* concerned with the practical use of their field of knowledge. On the other hand, home economists are concerned *as home economists* with the practical uses of scientific knowledge to control limited parts of the environment for the welfare of humankind. This is analagous to the practical use of scientific knowledge in other professions, such as medicine, social work, engineering, teaching, and counseling.

Among fields of study based upon science, we have those concerned with understanding and predicting (the basic sciences) and those concerned with understanding, predicting, and controlling (the applied sciences). This makes the over-all structure of the applied sciences more complex in that there is an additional kind of knowledge with which they must deal. For example, in medicine, where promotion of health and the alleviation of disease and pain are basic concerns, it is necessary but it is not sufficient to have basic scientific knowledge from physiology and anatomy about the function and structure of the heart, factors affecting its functioning, and the like. In order to accomplish the goal of alleviating pain and disease of the heart, professional people in medicine must, drawing in part from theoretical knowledge, develop an area of knowledge about both *what can be done* to alleviate a particular heart ailment and *how to accomplish the task*. This kind of knowledge is often called technical knowledge or technology; the skillful use of such knowledge in diagnosis and treatment involves craftsmanship.

Similarly, in home economics, if we are to accomplish some goal which we say is ours in controlling certain aspects of the environment for the welfare of mankind, we must have certain basic scientific or theoretical knowledge. However, we must also *produce* and *use* technical knowledge which will enable us (1) to diagnose intelligently the needs of mankind relevant to our goal and (2) to use techniques which will achieve the purpose in helping persons to control those aspects of the environment necessary and desirable. Thus, we will add a third area of thought to the over-all structure of home economics, calling it Technology and Craftsmanship. (See figure 3.)

Since the technological knowledge we need is determined by what we want to accomplish as home economists, Meta-Theory gives direction to

101

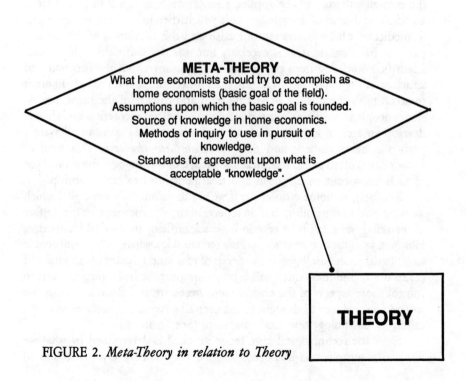

> **THEORY**
> Definitions of terms (concepts)
> Classifications of concepts
> Generalizations (showing relationships
>   between concepts)
> Theories (sets of generalizations and
>   definitions which explain other
>   generalizations)

FIGURE 1. *Home Economics Theory*

> **META-THEORY**
> What home economists should try to accomplish as
> home economists (basic goal of the field).
> Assumptions upon which the basic goal is founded.
> Source of knowledge in home economics.
> Methods of inquiry to use in pursuit of
> knowledge.
> Standards for agreement upon what is
> acceptable "knowledge".

> **THEORY**

FIGURE 2. *Meta-Theory in relation to Theory*

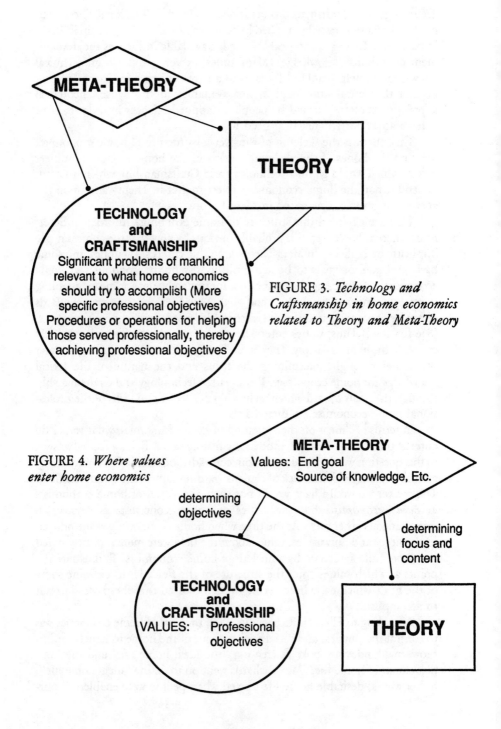

META-THEORY

THEORY

TECHNOLOGY and CRAFTSMANSHIP
Significant problems of mankind relevant to what home economics should try to accomplish (More specific professional objectives) Procedures or operations for helping those served professionally, thereby achieving professional objectives

FIGURE 3. *Technology and Craftsmanship in home economics related to Theory and Meta-Theory*

FIGURE 4. *Where values enter home economics*

META-THEORY
Values: End goal
Source of knowledge, Etc.

determining objectives

determining focus and content

TECHNOLOGY and CRAFTSMANSHIP
VALUES: Professional objectives

THEORY

Technology and Craftsmanship (as indicated by the directional line in our model). Because knowledge applied in Technology and Craftsmanship is drawn in part from Theory, theoretical knowledge available influences the development of technical knowledge. (Many times, however, concern for technical knowledge to help mankind leads us to a bare cupboard in Theory, in that needed theoretical knowledge is not available. In this sense, theoretical knowledge is often pursued by people in applied sciences in order to have it serve an important practical need.)

This, then, is the skeleton of the over-all structure of home economics. Meat on the bones of this skeleton consists of the home economics subject matter which would go into Technology and Craftsmanship, which, in turn, depends upon the home economics subject matter in Theory and upon the answers to questions accepted in Meta-Theory.

We have explored this structure of home economics in order to determine where values enter. It is probably obvious by now that the choices made implicitly or explicitly in Meta-Theory are value choices: (1) upholding some basic end goal or goals to be accomplished by home economists *as home economists,* (2) choosing the methods of inquiry to be used as means enabling home economists to reach their end goal(s), and (3) choosing the standards or modes of agreeing upon what is acceptable knowledge in home economics. (See figure 4.) Thus, values enter Theory through those assumed, explicitly or implicitly, in Meta-Theory. They enter Theory not as statements or postulates but rather through determining the focus and the nature of theoretical knowledge for home economics. Values enter Technology and Craftsmanship through the goals toward which technical knowledge and skills of the professional home economist are directed.

In terms of "meat on the skeleton" of home economics, what values do enter at these points? At this time in the history of our field, a factual answer to this question would reveal confusion, contradictions in the form of mutually exclusive values held, and lack of clarity regarding values held about the field. The answer we would have would not show the values of home economists *as home economists* but the values of home economists *as persons* in miscellaneous other roles. At the time when home economics was introduced into colleges and universities, values about the field were more explicitly stated and more fully agreed on by a nucleus of home economists. To illustrate the points at which values enter the structure of the field, let us examine some of the goals which early home economists indicated that the profession was to accomplish.

According to Ellen H. Richards in 1902, the goal of home economics was to control the physical and social environment of the home to benefit or improve mankind. She spoke of creating "the ideal home life" and the "improvement of home life." Mrs. Richards went on to define "ideal home life"; in her words, desirable home life existed when people were enabled to pur-

104

sue such "important and permanent interests" as "positive power of control of the mind to do what is demanded of it," "perfect control of the body and the perfect poise of . . . health," "zest in life, a new wish to make it of service," "freedom to live out" one's own life being "unhampered by traditions of the past," "due subordination (of things) to ideals" of person. (2, 3)

In 1901, Caroline L. Hunt expressed a similar concept of what home economics should accomplish: to secure through home life "freedom to create for oneself an external world corresponding to the world within." According to Miss Hunt, the securing of this freedom for the person through home life was dependent upon "the clearness with which he sees in the order of relative importance those things which have the power to affect life." Such freedom "presupposes knowledge—scientific knowledge." She valued the use of such knowledge in situations "in which the individual alone has power"; but, further, she saw value in the fact that "he can thru cooperation with other individuals change social conditions and thus increase his own and others' freedom." (4)

According to Alice A. Chown in 1902, home economics was, through "the study of the home," to create "new recognitions of the possibilities of humanity." She said: "Not only must the student of home economics constantly remember that the law of self-realization has been at work in all ages, but also that the influences that have molded society have affected the family, for it is an integral part of society. . . ." (5)

Such conceptions of what home economics should accomplish were values held—ends toward which action of home economists should be directed.

As has been indicated, early home economists valued scientific investigation as the source of knowledge. Mrs. Richards indicated that "home economics stands for . . . the utilization of all the resources of modern science to improve the home life." The 1902 Lake Placid Conference membership, in adopting a definition of home economics, indicated that it "is the study of [scientific] laws, conditions, principles and ideals which are concerned on the one hand with man's immediate physical environment and on the other hand with his nature as a social being, and . . . specially of the relation between those two factors." This selection of science as a source of knowledge was a value choice, for science was thereby considered a more desirable source than custom, tradition, exhortation, appeal to authority, or a priori thinking. In addition, scientific inquiry itself embodies a set of values. As Bronowski points out, "We can only practice science if we value truth" (6, p. 55). While the findings of science are neutral, the methods and standards of science are not at all neutral. Objectivity is more desirable than bias; independent thinking is preferable to dependence upon authority; openness to information is preferable to closed-mindedness; precision, to sloppiness in thinking; originality, to imitation; intellectual honesty, to dishonesty; and accuracy, to distortion.

These are illustrative of values which were once made explicit to the structure of home economics and which were viewed as elements of Meta-Home-Economics.

We have seen how values may be explicit or implicit. If it is true that home economists are not clear concerning values about the field and that the values which do exist are unrecognized assumptions, it is obvious that we cannot have explored justification and agreement concerning them. Let us turn now to the point of the significance of making our values explicit and of seeking agreement regarding our values as home economists.

Significance of Making Values Explicit and of Agreeing on Values About the Field

Let us look at the consequences of each of certain alternatives open to us: (1) the alternative of making our values explicit versus the alternative of leaving them implicit or unrecognized and (2) the alternative of seeking agreement versus the alternative of failing to seek agreement concerning our values.

Explicit versus implicit values. In speaking of his fellow psychologists, McLeod said, "No one can think or act without assumptions. There are those who try to make their philosophic assumptions explicit, and there are those who fail to recognize their assumptions. It is the latter who contribute most to our confusion" (7, p. 230). When our value assumptions, like any other, are made explicit, they are open to examination for their meaning and for their justification; when they are not made explicit, obviously our values go unexamined and justification cannot be attempted. Value assumptions made explicit are open to rational inquiry, to more adequate conceptualization, to consideration relative to existing conditions and knowledge available. Unrecognized and unexamined, values are irrational, ideationally inadequate, and dogmatic and absolute. Made explicit and rationally examined, values can become organized into a complex, consistent value orientation which characterizes those who achieve such an integration; according to studies of values, such a stage is reached by individuals and groups only through painful intellectual effort. Failure to recognize and clarify values makes us easy prey to self-contradictions and to lack of any basic orientation or purpose. Furthermore, it is only when values are made explicit that we can seek agreement regarding them. The preoccupation in recent years with what home economics is, with the quest for unity, with the role of home economics in higher education, with the organization of home economics in colleges and universities has its roots in the lack of a common clear goal or valued end for accomplishment for the field of home economics, in the failure to make our values explicit, and in not seeking agreement concerning our means and modes of action.

Seeking agreement versus failure to seek agreement upon values. Again, it is wise to emphasize that reference is not made to seeking agreement on *all* values, only about values which enter into the structure of home economics as a field. Furthermore, it should be noted that what is of concern is *seeking* agreement. There would seldom, if ever, be complete agreement among persons in a field of study. If agreement is reached in one area of value, it is time to move on to another to seek agreement there. In speaking of agreement, I do not mean agreement for the sake of agreement to be "nice" or "likeable" but conceptual agreement resulting from intellectually honest and complex thinking.

One of the conditions of rational inquiry is that those who are concerned with the inquiry enter into one another's minds, so to speak, for it is only in this way that we understand the thought back of what is said. We learn by honing our minds against the minds of others in rational inquiry. A necessary condition for such an encounter is the mutual assumption that, by keeping one's mind open and objectively exploring an area together long enough, we would come to see things in the same way; that is, we would agree. By agreeing to disagree, we abdicate the responsibility of the free and open mind; we run away from rational encounter to irrationally protect two or more closed minds. Agreeing to disagree is one alternative to seeking agreement. The only other alternative is despair or skepticism, neither of which contributes to productivity. As Pole points out, "It is possible in seeking agreement to recognize the existence of different views, to explain them and to search for ways of resolving them; here rationality gets a toehold and the process of inquiry is put in motion." (8, p. 87)

When we fail to seek agreement, we often turn home economics into a convenient personal career rather than a professional field toward which we make corporately responsible contributions. Members of a professional field form a social group, a small subcultural or social system. To share in the culture or social system is to share ways of thinking and working. When these shared ways of thinking and working form a core of common values, the effect is one of integration. Assuming that these values have been agreed upon through discursive reason in seeking agreement, productivity of the field is enhanced. The goals of the fields are not only more clearly defined; they are more adequately accomplished. When agreement on a core of common values is weak or nonexistent, the effect is one of disintegration. Concerted effort toward making the social system productive is minimal; and then, of course, productivity is reduced, if not completely curtailed.

It is common within a social system for the older members to induct the younger members into the values of the culture. However, this can only operate in a culture where values are clearly explicit. It is obvious that this condition does not exist in home economics today. Here is a place where experienced

107

and less-experienced home economists need to seek agreement through discursive reason if home economics is to be the integrated and productive profession it started out to be.

References

1. Kluckhohn, C. Values and Value-Orientations in the Theory of Action. In *Toward a General Theory of Action*, T. Parsons and E. A. Shils (Editors). Cambridge, Massachusetts: Harvard University Press, 1951, pp. 388-433.

2. Hunt, C. L. *The Life of Ellen H. Richards.* Washington, D.C.: American Home Economics Association, 1958.

3. *Lake Placid Conference on Home Economics. Proceedings of Conferences 1 to 10, 1899-1908.* Washington, D.C.: American Home Economics Association. Proceedings of the first, second, and third conferences, 1899-1901, pp. 7, 13, 24, 70-71.

4. Hunt, C. L. Revaluations. In *Lake Placid Conference on Home Economics. Proceedings of Conferences 1 to 10, 1899-1908.* Washington, D.C.: American Home Economics Association. Proceedings of the first, second, and third conferences, 1899-1901, pp. 79-89.

5. Chown, A. A. Effect of Some Social Changes on the Family. In *Lake Placid Conference on Home Economics. Proceedings of Conferences 1 to 10, 1899-1908.* Washington, D.C.: American Home Economics Association. Proceedings of the fourth annual conference, 1902, pp. 31-35.

6. Bronowski, J. The Values of Science. In *New Knowledge in Human Values,* A. H. Maslow (Editor). New York: Harper & Brothers, 1959, pp. 52-64.

7. McLeod, R. B. Person Perception: A Commentary. In *Perspectives in Personality Research,* H. P. Davis and J. C. Brengelmann (Editors). New York: Springer Publishing Company, 1960, pp. 226-244.

8. Pole, D. *Conditions of Rational Inquiry.* London: The Athlone Press, 1961.

14

The Imperatives of Change for Home Economics

Earl J. McGrath
Director of the Institute of Higher Education

As the opening address of the 59th AHEA annual meeting on June 25, 1968, in Minneapolis, Dr. McGrath reported on the study of the future role and scope of home economics conducted by the Institute of Higher Education at the instigation of the home economics professional section and the executive committee of the National Association of State Universities and Land-Grant Colleges. Because this study is having such an impact on projections of future needs in home economics, Dr. McGrath's address is printed in full here along with the question-and-answer panel that followed, even though there is some repetition of the preliminary report to the Association of Administrators of Home Economics, which was published in the February 1968 *Journal.*

Let me begin with a confession. When the representatives of the profession of home economics and the officers of the Carnegie Corporation asked the Institute of Higher Education to undertake a study of home economics in the National Association of State Universities and Land-Grant Colleges, I had some hesitation about undertaking such a project. My reluctance stemmed from the specific nature of the mission which was to make a study aimed primarily at defining the future role and scope of home economics in the member institutions. This was not an unusual request. The Institute had made comparable investigations of a dozen or more other professional schools such as engineering, business administration, and nursing.

In none of these, however, was there any question about the continuing existence of a particular type of professional educational unit which prepared practitioners for a specific occupation. No matter how radically some may have felt that a given kind of professional education ought to be reshaped, there was no suggestion that it ought to be abandoned or scattered among other educational units. With home economics it was different.

There were discouraging statements by some who, even though they were not as well informed as one could wish, nevertheless were responsible persons. A few felt that although the home economics units in our colleges and universities had performed service of unquestionable value in the past, their principal goals had been reached. The very reason for the continued existence of home economics units was, therefore, called into question. Some members of the profession themselves, doubtless unwittingly, gave support to this view by questioning whether home economists had exerted the leadership necessary to keep the profession abreast of the emerging needs of society. Hence, some educators outside the profession believed that the schools and departments concerned with home economics would eventually wither and disappear, and should be allowed to do so. Except for the obstacles which such persons may put in the way of future developments, I felt that this group of extremists could be disregarded; for the facts indicate that the demand for home economists will increase indefinitely. Today there are about 90,000 individuals employed in home economics occupations in the United States. About 55 percent of these persons teach some branch of the subject in schools and colleges. Another 30 percent are in dietetics; between 5 and 6 percent are employed in business, industry, or associations; and 5 percent are in Cooperative Extension Service work.

These fields of teaching, dietetics, business, and Extension will doubtless continue to absorb a preponderant proportion of the future graduates of schools of home economics. But even these established careers will not remain static in their functions. Moreover, new types of occupations for which a higher education in home economics will be the primary preparation will continue to come into being. Hence, the existing and prospective employment opportunities in home economics will be transformed by the major social trends of internationalism and expanded social welfare.

Let me assure you at once, therefore, that the findings in this study indicate that there will be no lessening in the need for individuals trained in the skills of the home economics occupations. On the contrary, in the foreseeable future the demand for both generalists and specialists in the occupations related to home economics will continue to grow in response to internationalism, population shifts, and welfare trends. But if these new demands for additional persons in these occupations and in American society generally are to be met, extensive expansion and reorganization of education in the field of home economics are unavoidable. In responding to these forces of change, the profession and the institutions concerned will have to adapt traditional practices to the creative organization of new programs. The changing conditions of life and social trends make it impossible to meet the new opportunities simply by pursuing old ideals and goals more efficiently.

But another school of thought about the future of home economics, it seems to me, deserves more serious consideration. This view holds that the various instructional, research, and community services rendered by home economics could be performed more effectively by other branches of our institutions of higher education. At first blush there is some logic in such a proposal. If young people in schools of home economics need to know about dietetics, why shouldn't they attend courses in the medical school or in the department of chemistry? Likewise, why should not the department of psychology offer all the instruction in child growth and development; the department of economics, courses in consumer economics; and the department of art, courses in home decoration; and so on through the complete curricular offerings in home economics? Presumably, under this plan a student majoring in home economics would simply follow a composite program of instruction drawn largely if not wholly from other departmental units. Marjorie East, a member of the accreditation committee of the American Home Economics Association, has stated the rationale for this position in these sentences:

> The question remains. What is home economics? Within the field there is disagreement, even though we give tacit approval to such unifying statements as those appearing in *New Directions*. Is home economics a single field? A collection of subject-matter areas related primarily by the loosening ties of historical association? Is there anything gained by holding onto and strengthening the commonalities? Is more to be gained by cutting the ties and setting off separately for our destinies—as dietitians, nursery school teachers, textile technologists, clothing psychologists, family relations counselors, to name a few of the specializations?[1]

And one of the persons who collaborated in an earlier study of home economics done by the Institute states the position even more pointedly when he says:

> The question which may then be legitimately raised is whether the various sub-specialties loosely grouped in home economics might not gain by being regrouped with other curriculums. Psychologists, sociologists, social workers, and educators are frequently as much concerned with problems in the home and family area as home economists are. Architects, engineers, landscape architects, and others can contribute to house planning and household equipment. After such regrouping, it might become desirable or necessary to organize inter-disciplinary teams to deal with pervasive problems of the home and family at some new and higher level than is possible at present.[2]

[1]Marjorie East, What is home economics? *J. Home Econ.* **57** (May 1965), p. 387.
[2]Paul L. Dressel, *The Undergraduate Curriculum in Higher Education.* Washington, D.C.: The Center for Applied Research in Education, 1963, p. 65.

Speech instructors will tell you never to begin an address on a negative note of the kind I have just struck. I have risked doing so for several reasons: First, we ought to recognize that the future of home economics will be determined by the clear and realistic way in which we answer the questions raised. And second, because I want to say at the outset that to the informed observer, like myself, from outside the profession these arguments don't hold water. On the other hand, they ought to shock all interested persons into the recognition that merely tinkering with the curriculum, or with the administrative organization, or with the admissions standards will not assure a flourishing future for home economics. These are innocuous—and I may add wasteful— pleasures which many other professional schools and subject-matter departments may and sometimes do enjoy, but for home economics they may be perilous. Only a searching review of the purposes of home economics, its teaching functions, its research programs, and its public services in the light of the social conditions of our time will fill the present requirements.

If our study provides the basic information for such a review and suggests certain lines of future development, it will have served its purpose. In the last analysis, however, only the profession can assure its healthy future by dedicating itself to a continuing review of the purposes and programs of home economics in terms of the emerging social needs. Only thus can the profession enjoy an esteemed position in the larger enterprise of American higher education.

Some Major Findings

Time is not available today to review even all the major findings and recommendations in our report, which is now in print and, therefore, easily available to anyone who wants to study it in detail.[3] At this time I want to talk about a few of the major findings and the issues they raise and suggest how they might be dealt with. Take first the character and the structure of the instructional program. Instead of splitting the field up and scattering the pieces over other departments and disciplines as has been suggested, the curricula in home economics ought to become more clearly identifiable wholes with an integrity of their own. It is difficult to see how this objective can be reached except where there is a discrete home economics unit with an administrator of its own reporting to the top academic officer. This type of

[3]Earl J. McGrath and Jack T. Johnson, *The Changing Mission of Home Economics*. Teachers College Press, Columbia University, New York, N.Y. 10027, 122 pp., $3.50.

organization has already been accomplished in some places but not universally by any means. The faculty, in turn, should make its own academic decisions, construct its own program, and set its own requirements for degrees consistent with the general regulations of the institution.

Instead of sending its students to other departments for specialized instruction, the home economics unit ought to provide most of its own courses. Home economics students should, of course, receive instruction in basic courses pursued generally by undergraduates in such fields as English, mathematics, physical science, and social science in the appropriate departments. But in the areas of knowledge which compose the special branches of home economics, instruction should be provided by the faculty of home economics and from a specific "angle of vision." The reason for this curricular arrangement is related to the fact that the advanced and abstruse theory propounded in most disciplines has no observable relation to the ordinary problems of life. This situation has caused one psychologist of national repute to make the shocking observation that a teacher who took a course in learning theory in the psychology department would probably gain little knowledge helpful in dealing with the everyday problems of the classroom. If students in home economics are to receive instruction relevant to the goals they are pursuing related to dietetics, child psychology, home decoration, consumer economics, or marriage and the family, then the preponderance of this teaching must be done by those who are able to relate the theoretical substance of these various disciplines to the matters with which those who graduate in home economics may be expected to deal.

This does not mean that members of home economics faculties should offer the same long sequences in various specialized fields already available elsewhere. One of the disturbing features of the curricula in all university divisions is the irresistible tendency to split up the subject matter into narrower and narrower units, each of which becomes a part of an extensive sequence. The result is that those who do not wish to become specialists in the field cannot gain an introduction suitable to their more limited purposes. Furthermore, it does not mean that home economics faculties should not establish working relationships with other units, which would prevent needless duplication or make possible new cooperative efforts. It does mean that programs in home economics if they are to be justified as separate academic entities will have to have identifiable purposes and a wholeness of their own.

This leads me to comment on some aspects of undergraduate instruction in home economics, which ought to be related to several developments in the mainstream of professional education. They can be summed up in the statement that all types of professional education are becoming more general. In the older professions of law and medicine, of course, most candidates for admission to the professional school already have had a substantial nonprofessional general education in a college of liberal arts. But the other professions which still offer undergraduate degrees are moving in the same direction by increasing the proportion of nonprofessional subjects in their curricula and by reducing the number of undergraduate specialized majors. In the undergraduate engineering programs, for example, the proportion of courses in the arts and sciences has been rising steadily. The practice at MIT and at Carnegie Tech, to name only two requiring extensive instruction in the social sciences and the humanities, is now being extended generally in engineering schools. Moreover, even in the technical specialties the curriculum is becoming more general. In some engineering schools it has been decided to offer no undergraduate major in chemical, mechanical, civil, or aeronautical engineering. A general foundation in the engineering and related sciences is laid in the undergraduate years, and those who expect to specialize in these fields must expect to take graduate work in the appropriate specialized departments. Programs of instruction in such fields as business administration, nursing, journalism, and social work all reveal the same general trends. The implications for home economics are clear. To the degree that the field wishes to move with the mainstream of higher education, it will find it necessary to require a broad base of nonprofessional instruction, keep the range of specialized undergraduate majors at a minimum, and require at least a fifth year of study for those who expect to follow a professional career for much of their lives.

Since there has been some misunderstanding about the connotation of the term "general education" as used in the report, I wish to try to be more precise about its meaning. It was not our intention to suggest that home economics students should necessarily pursue broad survey courses in the various disciplines which were popular some years ago, although some very exciting interdisciplinary innovations are still being tried. We merely wish to suggest that a considerable proportion of the undergraduate major ought to be composed of instruction outside of the specialized branches of home economics. The graduates in general home economics and in teaching make up half or more of the whole. This may present a dilemma for college departments or schools of home economics. If home economics pursues a specialized and professional approach, it may neglect the generalist and liberal approach so necessary for the training of secondary teachers and for those who do not intend to spend their lives as professional practitioners. A program composed of a collection of specialties is quite different from one made up of a professional major supported by a large unit of nontechnical subject matter. Home economics must decide whether it wishes to be a field with a common core of general education and a common core of professional education with a modest number of undergraduate specialized majors or whether it wishes to be a collection of disparate specializations with little in common and clustered around the rather nebulous concept of "home and family life."

Need for Interdisciplinary Research

Another issue the profession must deal with realistically is the place of research in the whole enterprise of home economics. One fact our study made undeniably clear. The amount of research presently done by the staffs in schools of home economics is extremely limited. Moreover, it is concentrated in a few institutions and also concentrated in the field of nutrition. The dominance of research in nutrition is revealed in the fact that at the time of the study, of the 533 sponsored research projects then under way, 42 percent were in foods and nutrition. In less than 20 percent of all projects was the home economics staff collaborating with researchers in other departments, and in about half of these scattered interdepartmental research efforts agriculture was the other department involved. It was not our intention to depreciate the established research programs in nutrition. Nevertheless, it is clear that the opportunities for interdisciplinary research involving home economics in fruitful cooperation with other disciplines, particularly in the natural sciences, still remain unexploited. Home economics, to be sure, can and ought to contribute its own unique orientation or angle of vision to research involving the family and home life; but in order to assure that the investigations undertaken possess both substance and broad significance, it is essential that working relationships be established with productive scholars in other disciplines. There is abundant evidence to show that the most fruitful new ideas in many other fields of knowledge, and their application to human problems, often come from individuals who are working on projects which border on fields other than their own specialty and who view problems from a "marginal" perspective. Many of these outside explorers have brought to their research a novel orientation which has produced the most arresting, innovative ideas and procedures.

A further striking fact about the research activities of home economists is the concentration of doctoral programs in a few institutions. Our study indicates that at the doctoral level approximately ten universities have produced most of the personnel for college teaching and research in home economics. This pattern may change as more universities are urged to offer doctoral programs. In the years ahead, however, the profession and society as a whole will be better served if this advanced instruction continues to be concentrated in a limited number of institutions. There is no convincing evidence at present that for home economists to succeed outside of college teaching—for example, in business or industry—they will be required in the near future to earn the doctorate or, for that matter, the master's degree. It is an established fact that offering a quality program in teaching or research at the doctoral level is one of the most costly undertakings any institution can become involved in. Moreover, a severely limited graduate program with inadequate staff and facilities may result in superficiality or provincial inquiries of little scholarly significance. Most important, however, it does not seem likely at present that the demand for doctorates in home economics will expand beyond the capacities of present institutions to produce them. Hence, expansion in the number of doctoral programs can properly be delayed unless there is a clearly unsatisifed need among the constituency and unless the substantial resources are available to meet the need at a suitable academic level.

At the master's level, however, a number of institutions could expand their activities to include graduate study and research dealing with practical problems in the various divisions of home economics education. The research and development programs of the nation now involve annual expenditures of billions of dollars. A substantial proportion of these funds are used to support so-called "pure" research, but it is no exaggeration to say that the dramatic developments in science and technology flow from the application of theoretical knowledge to the practical problems of our economy and our social life. It should not be necessary, in the light of these advances, to argue that much larger expenditures of thought, effort, and money on the practical problems which fall within the purview of home economics would result in comparable benefits to society at large.

Expanding Needs In Social Areas

In a similar way, we ought to consider the relationship between home economics and the social revolution occurring in our society. No documentation is needed to justify the statement that the causes of the present turbulent disturbances lie in the conditions of life among the underprivileged, the minority groups, the under-educated, the inadequately housed and fed, and to a large extent those who live in the center city. No one seems wise enough to provide a completely comprehensive master plan for raising the level of living in these centers by eliminating the basic causes of poverty, ignorance, and dissatisfaction. Strenuous efforts already being made and others envisaged will doubtless bear rich fruit in the days ahead. My purpose in alluding to these matters here is to state unequivocally and clearly that whatever projects are undertaken to improve the conditions of life in the urban centers ought to involve those prepared in the field of home economics. In the improvement of education, housing, health, welfare, the family—in all these areas of living and many others as well—the home economists have an obvious and, in some respects, a unique contribution to make. Typically they will have to assume this role in association with other members of a team drawn from other professions, such as health and social welfare. There are, to be sure, examples of such cooperative participation by home economists, but the number is too limited.

116

Several years ago, of 108 cities with a population of 100,000 or more only 16 employed home economists on the staffs of their welfare departments, and only 17 state welfare departments involved home economists in their activities. With a few exceptions, the employment of home economists for work in the inner city is probably not appreciably greater today. The reasons for this failure of public agencies to use a professional resource of obvious value were too far removed from the thrust of our main inquiry to permit an exhaustive investigation. The members of the profession will be interested to know, however, that discussions have already been held with the officers of the Carnegie Corporation, which will probably eventuate in an expansion of our study into this very area. We believe that more precise data should be gathered concerning the involvement of home economists in social welfare programs in the urban centers. We should know why their unique abilities have not been used more extensively and what needs to be done to change the existing situation. If additional training of a type not now generally provided, is needed to prepare home economists for a fuller service in urban centers, we should know what this is and how it can best be provided on a crash basis for those who could move into such activities at once, and under a more permanent plan for those who are now in the undergraduate programs. In any event, some exploratory activities have already begun and are likely to be expanded during the summer months.

It may be that in order to achieve the changes necessary for this expanded service existing laws relating to the training and use of home economists will have to be revised. For reasons which home economists well know, many of their programs have historically had an agricultural orientation. When the first applicable federal statutes were passed, a very substantial proportion of the families of the United States lived in rural districts. These families needed the services which home economists could provide, especially through Cooperative Extension. Rural life has been immeasurably enriched through these services. No thoughtful persons would wish to see curtailed or eliminated those which are still appropriate and needed.

The fact is, however, that today our population is preponderantly urban. One population expert predicts that 80 percent of the people of the United States will live in cities by the 1980's and 90 percent by the year 2000. If home economists are to continue to serve the families of this country on a broad basis they will have to shift their orientation away from the farm to the town. Not only that—the same people moving into the city will face different problems of housing, eating, raising families, and working. These problems can be alleviated in part by the use of the knowledge and the skills of home economists, just as the lives of their forebears on the farm were enriched by an earlier generation of the profession. Today, the knowledge encompassed within home economics must be made available in more ways to more people.

If one views the changed circumstances of American life, it is clear that the legislation and the state and federal agreements that undergird home economics education, Extension, and research are becoming increasingly inadequate. They do not allow home economics enough latitude to meet the changing needs of society, nor do they sufficiently stimulate those concerned to inaugurate these changes. Specifically, the purpose and mission of home economics as set forth in legislative acts should be re-examined in the light of the changing conditions of modern life brought about by scientific and technological advance. Because the poor and the minority groups in the cities are the least informed about the ways in which their homes, their employability, their health, and their children's well-being can be enhanced, legislative reform should center on extending home economics programs to the inner city.

International Needs

Lastly, home economists have become increasingly aware of the need for their services in many of the newly created nations in which education and public service are as yet undeveloped. Yet, the profession ought to be more broadly and more deeply involved in the international fields. It is significant that out of the 12,600 Peace Corps volunteers who had gone overseas by April 1967 only 95 had majored in home economics and only 119 in nutrition—a combined total of only 1.7 percent of the entire Corps overseas.

Home economists can make at least four approaches to meet the new emerging opportunities overseas: (1) they can offer programs to more foreign specialists; (2) they can go abroad to help educators in other lands develop home economics programs in their schools and universities; (3) they can train individuals for overseas duty; and (4) they can promote the intercultural exchange of professional home economists.

Much more could be said to substantiate the claim that a new and exciting day lies ahead for the professional home economist. Our report supplies statistics and other forms of information to support the contention that schools of home economics, if properly supported and encouraged, can greatly enhance their already substantial contribution to the productiveness, the well-being, and the happiness of our people as well as those in other lands. In order to achieve these broader and higher levels of service, the profession will need the understanding and the support of other educators, of the highest officers of the government, and of those who are the beneficiaries of its services. And in the last analysis, the destiny of the profession rests with the members of the profession itself. If the leadership in the American Home Economics Association will clearly set forth professional goals and dynamically organize to achieve them, the profession will continue to grow in stature and in the respect of the whole fraternity of education. More importantly, this will assure the further enrichment of American life and the well-being of our people.

So I end my experiences in connection with this study, not in any doubt about the future of home economics but in the firm conviction that the schools which train the professionals in this field will grow in size, in strength, and in position in the larger enterprise of American higher education.

15

The Changing Mission
of Home Economics

Earl J. McGrath
Director of the Institute of Higher Education
Teacher's College
Columbia University

This report by Dr. McGrath represents the culmination of many years of effort on the part of home economics administrators. In 1959 the Home Economics Division asked the executive committee of the National Association of State Universities and Land-Grant Colleges to support a study of the "problems, objectives, and future of home economics" in their member institutions. Frances Zuill of the University of Wisconsin, Helen Canoyer of Cornell University, and I were appointed to work with President David Henry of the University of Illinois and Chancellor John Caldwell of North Carolina State University at Raleigh in preparing the study proposal and obtaining the funds. Later President Novice Fawcett of Ohio State University replaced Chancellor Caldwell.

In 1964 the Carnegie Corporation agreed to support the study and the Institute of Higher Education of Teachers College, Columbia University, contracted to conduct it. Earl McGrath, director of the Institute and director of the study, made this report to the Association of Administrators of Home Economics (successor to the Home Economics Division of the NASULGC) at its annual meeting in Chicago on November 10, 1967. The complete report will be ready for distribution by the Teachers College Press later this spring.

Helen R. LeBaron
Iowa State University

For some time clinicians who have worked in prenatal clinics throughout the South have been aware of incredibly high rates of iron-deficiency anemia among some groups of pregnant Negro women. The cause of this anemia has been tracked to a tradition extending back to slavery: that of eating clay. This practice, which has been passed on from one generation to another, aids in killing hunger pains and—according to folklore—is beneficial during pregnancy both in preventing nausea and venereal disease as well as in providing increased nutrition.

Recently in New York City physicians have been discovering a number of cases of iron-deficiency anemia among patients from Harlem, who, it turns out, also follow this same practice with one modification: the substitution of laundry starch for clay when clay is unavailable. It is now becoming evident that among pregnant Negro women in the metropolitan area the eating of laundry starch—as much as two pounds a day—and resultant anemia is not uncommon, even among those who have gone to school in New York and have lived in the city all of their lives.

How is it that in the final third of the twentieth century, in the most affluent society in the world and within blocks of famous medical centers and educational institutions, such pitiful misunderstanding of human health and nutrition exists? How has information about food values and diet failed to reach these people? And who is responsible for the resulting malady when bone marrow of mothers and children contains no iron?

This public health problem cannot be solved by merely disseminating information on good nutrition: it requires effort to overcome cultural and value differences between disadvantaged Negroes and middle-class whites. However, there is no question that this social problem as well as other problems of health, social services, and family life indicate that the professions have failed to bring their knowledge about human life effectively to bear on the lives of human beings, both in the ghettos of the metropolis and the back country of rural America.

Many home economists—like their associates in public health, social welfare, and counseling services—are aware of these problems and seek to overcome them. They are asking why the field of home economics cannot play a more active role in the solution of social problems. Teachers and administrators within the field, as well as individuals outside, share a concern that the content and the philosophy of home economics have not adequately adjusted to population shifts from rural to urban environments, to the increasingly rapid tempo of change in our own society, and to the expanded role of American aid and technology in international life. For some years they have wanted to examine university home economics programs in order to determine whether these programs need redefinition or redirection to prepare their students for useful and satisfying work in tomorrow's world. Their farsighted concern has been particularly evident among the leaders of institutions represented at this meeting of home economics administrators.

As a result of this concern, some five years ago the executive committee of the National Association of State Universities and Land-Grant Colleges proposed—at the request of the Home Economics Division—a study aimed at defining the future role and scope of home economics in the member institutions of the Association. Representatives of these organizations asked the officers of the Carnegie Corporation of New York to support such an inquiry and the Institute of Higher Education to conduct it. Discussions among the persons concerned led to a grant from the Carnegie Corporation, and during the past two academic years the study has been carried forward with the unreserved cooperation of home economists.

During the course of the study, the staff of the Institute has had the experienced counsel of an advisory committee consisting of representatives from home economics, business, university administration, and the field of higher education in general. This committee met five times while the study was in progress, and at its final meeting on October 6, 1967 its members unanimously supported the conclusions and recommendations which will be discussed in this presentation and more fully in the report being published this spring. Throughout this study and especially in its proposals the dominant goal has been the improvement of the practice of home economics and the expansion of its established and potential beneficial influences on American society. Now let me present some relevant facts and then make a necessarily abridged presentation of the principal conclusions and recommendations.

Opportunities for Graduates of Home Economics Programs

First, a few facts about the scope and character of the home economics enterprise. Today there are about 90,000 individuals employed in home economics occupations in the United States. About 55 percent of these persons teach some branch of this subject in schools and colleges. Another 30 percent are in dietetics; between 5 and 6 percent are employed in business, industry, or associations; and 5 percent are in Cooperative Extension work.

These fields of teaching, dietetics, business, and Extension will doubtless continue to absorb a preponderant proportion of the future graduates of schools of home economics. But even these established careers will not remain static in their functions. Moreover, new types of occupations for which a higher education in home economics will be the primary preparation will continue to come into being. Hence, the existing and prospective employment opportunities in home economics will be transformed by the major social trends of internationalism, urbanism, and expanded social welfare.

Examples of ways in which these developments in modern life are modifying home economics careers can be found since the end of World War II in the new missions in international service performed by home economists in improving child care, nutrition, home life, and the productivity of families in the newly developing countries. Several conferences have already been held under AAHE auspices to sketch the future functions of home economics in the international sphere. The profession can take several approaches to meet these emerging international opportunities: (1) The land-grant colleges and state universities can attract to their programs in home economics more specialists in the field from other lands; (2) they can send more American members of the profession abroad to help educators in other countries to develop home economics programs in their own schools and universities; (3) they can train home economists specifically for overseas duty, either on a temporary basis as, for example, in the Peace Corps, or for more permanent careers; and (4) they can promote the intercultural exchange of professional home economists. No precise estimate can be made of the number of home economics graduates who might be engaged in international activities. This is because of the swiftly changing conditions of life today and because the demand for such service will doubtless rise with the increasing availability of trained personnel. No informed person can doubt, however, that the existing supply could unquestionably be multiplied several times over and yet not meet the prospective demand.

Not only have increases in the world's population and the rising expectations of a better life thrust additional responsibilities upon home economists but also the growth in the size and the mobile character of our own population here at home call for expanded and more varied services from home economists.

The steady progression of urbanization is shaking many American universities out of their rural orientation and turning their attention toward the problems of the cities. This trend gives every sign of continuing indefinitely. It has been estimated, for example, that 85 percent of the young people growing up on farms today will in their productive adult years earn their livelihoods in nonagricultural pursuits. It is estimated that by the year 2000 the 3.5 million farmers in the United States today will drop to one million. During the same period the population density in the metropolitan regions may rise from approximately 400 to 700 persons per square mile. These changes in the place of residence of our people as a whole do not imply that institutions of higher education can or should neglect the educational and social needs of our rural citizens, whose contributions to our growing national well-being have been incalculable, but it does mean that more attention must be given to the lives and problems of the millions who, unlike their fathers and mothers, will live in the cities.

Hence, as members of the home economics profession have already observed, the Extension services that in the past enriched and enhanced farm life must assist in the enormously complex and urgent problems connected with making life in the cities more productive, more enlightened, and more satisfying personally. Members of the profession will have to serve more people than ever before and in a greater variety of ways through community centers, high schools, community colleges, and public television. And to meet these emerging conditions the content of Extension programs must continue to change, emphasizing such aspects of our national life as consumer education, resource management, mental health, and social development. Home economists will be called on to assist in problems ranging from nourishment and home repair to sanitation and family stability. Inevitably, these activities of home economists will border on and overlap those of other service professions, such as social work, public health, family counseling, and nursing, to mention only four. The need is great for home economists trained in urban Extension techniques and equipped to work with these other professionals, and here again the supply falls far short of the demand.

In summary, let me assure you that the findings in this study indicate that there will be no lessening of the need for individuals trained in the skills of the home economics occupations. On the contrary, in the visible future the demand for both generalists and specialists in the occupations related to home economics will continue to grow in response to internationalism, population shifts, and welfare trends. But if these new demands for additional persons in these occupations and in American society generally are to be met, extensive expansion and reorganization of education in the field of home economics is unavoidable. In responding to these forces of change, the profession and the institutions concerned will have to adapt traditional practices to the creative organization of new programs. The changing conditions of life and social trends make it impossible to meet the new opportunities simply by pursuing old ideals and goals more efficiently. Instead, the ideals and goals of home economics and the means for achieving them must change and expand with opportunities.

Change in Home Economics Education

Before setting forth explicitly the changes that seem to be desirable in education in home economics, it may be helpful to formulate a few basic concepts about the field as a whole. Home economics is not a profession with a single distinct body of knowledge, skills, and ethics. Like the whole of the education enterprise, home economics is an area of human interest and concern that encompasses and impinges on a number of occupations and other life activities. Its central mission has been and must continue to be that of *family service*. This focus of effort is not only appropriate but preferable to any other presently conceivable alternative. From the beginning, the preoccupation of home economists has been centered in the family as the milieu in which individuals grow and achieve their basic learning in preparation for a productive, rewarding, and satisfying life.

Around this commitment to the family unit there have been a number of more specific purposes related to such matters as nutrition, dietetics, and institutional management directed either to individual needs or to groups other than the family. Yet "family service" remains the integrative center of home economics, just as "patient care" forms the core of nursing.

Our study has attempted to find out how in the future the social trends of American life will affect this dominant concern of the field with the family and what effect these developments should have on home economics education. In this review attention has been given especially to courses and curricula in the field, to Extension services, and to research. The conclusions reached in this study about these three functions of programs in home economics constitute the remainder of this report.

The curriculum. Considering first courses and curricula, it is abundantly clear that in the future the knowledge encompassed within home economics must be made available in more ways to more people. Systematic, formalized instruction in degree programs will obviously be required. But major media such as newspapers, magazines, and television will have to be used more extensively for the wider transmission of useful knowledge and skills. Citizens generally have the right to knowledge about matters of such crucial importance to their own well-being and that of their families. Hence, lectures, workshops, and credit and non-credit courses on problems encompassed within home economics should increasingly be offered to individuals of all ages and both sexes through a variety of educational institutions—community centers, public schools, colleges and universities. Community colleges, especially, ought to play a prominent role in the future in providing such educational services, for in many population centers these colleges appear likely to have major responsibility for providing a wide variety of adult and continuing education. At these institutions young people—regardless of economic background, race, or sex—increasingly will also be given an opportunity for a college education to the full extent of their ability to profit from it. Thus, it seems likely that more and more men and women will want and should receive instruction in home economics as part of their general education, as a leisure-time pursuit in continuing education, or as preparation for a career.

But although these opportunities for students to enroll in home economics courses will undoubtedly increase in the future, we do not believe that an increasing proportion of college students will *major* in home economics. On the contrary, women—who even now constitute 99 percent of the college graduates in home economics—are entering more diversified fields of employment, and as a result the proportion majoring in home economics will probably continue to decline. This relative shrinkage of the field will be proportionate to the efforts home economics educators make in identifying new career opportunities and in designing suitable preparation for them.

Perhaps paradoxically, then, while increasing numbers of schools and colleges should make *service courses* in home economics areas available to their students, fewer of them in the future will, or indeed should, offer a *major concentration* in the field. In particular, many liberal arts colleges that now offer home economics with inadequate faculties and facilities should consider dropping their degree programs. If they continue these programs, more of them should attempt to obtain appropriate instruction in home economics through consortia or cooperative programs with nearby universities. If the programs in many of the liberal arts colleges are dropped or offered cooperatively and enrollments in public institutions generally continue to soar, the state colleges and universities will inevitably play an increasingly major role in preparing home economists. Already the institutions of this administrators association graduate over half of the nation's bachelor's candidates and two-thirds of the master's candidates in home economics. Their influence in home economics vis-a-vis the private colleges will inevitably expand.

When you look at the curricula of your institutions, it is obvious that specialized majors within home economics at the undergraduate level will continue to be necessary, if only because of society's need for such specialized skills as those in dietetics and nutrition. In fact, although these specialties have grown up under the umbrella of home economics, it seems inevitable and natural that as they continue to mature their ties with the central concern of home economics—family service—will become attenuated. In some instances programs parallel to home economics will spring up and eventually become independent of it.

While problems involving these specialized majors require attention, the primary need of undergraduate home economics programs at this time is to assure the quality of the *broad, unspecialized* major in the field—the major that is needed by students who enroll in order to become better homemakers or more effective community volunteer workers or who seek employment as high school teachers or home economists in business. This broad curriculum, which appears in danger of being relegated to a position below the specialized curricula, is in magnitude at least the most important of all. At present, nearly three-fourths of all home economics degrees are awarded in the unspecialized curricula of home economics education or general home economics.

Such curricula fulfill a genuine need for generalists in home economics and avoid the dangers of overspecialization. As John Gardner has pointed out,

> . . . there are many tasks that can be effectively performed only by men and women who have retained some capacity to function as generalists— leadership and management, certain kinds of innovation, communication and teaching and many of the responsibilities of child-rearing and of citizenship. Furthermore, the extremely specialized man may lose the adaptability so essential in a changing world. He may be unable to reorient himself when technological changes make his specialty obsolete.[1]

[1]John W. Gardner, *Self-Renewal: The Individual and the Innovative Society.* New York: Harper & Row, 1963, p. 24.

And whether the students who pursue this major choose it to improve their skills as a spouse or parent or professionally as a businesswoman or a teacher, it can and should provide for them a liberal education in the best sense of the word—where liberality is, in Samuel Alexander's words, "a spirit of pursuit, not a choice of subject." For this reason, *home economics as an undergraduate major can best confirm its heritage and meet present challenges by retaining a strong generalist major and expanding its interdisciplinary base in order to fully comprehend contemporary social problems and those of family life.*

The Institute of Higher Education has made exhaustive studies of curricular changes since the Second World War in other fields, such as business administration, engineering, professional art and music, nursing, and education. In all other occupationally oriented undergraduate programs the purposes and the content have been becoming more general, both in the sense that the proportion of nonprofessional subject matter has been increasing and that professional instruction itself is becoming more broad-gauged. Thus, if home economists wish to move in the mainstream of professional education in the United States, the basic undergraduate program in home economics must be broadened. This curriculum for students who will serve as generalists in home economics rather than in its specialties must consist of a systematic and interdisciplinary major rather than a congeries of snippets of specialization. Its instructional core should be related to an analysis of family structure and functioning; its value orientation should be that of assistance to families; and its goal, the creation and enhancement of viable family life. These integrating principles provide the unity of concepts, skills, and values that are distinctive to home economics. Without them the generalist major will dissolve into chameleon-like eclecticism and the specialist majors into mere technical preparation for specific jobs which have a way of becoming outdated in a few years.

Since the scope of concern of this undergraduate major ranges from human development to consumer economics, its content must be closely integrated with the basic analytic disciplines, such as biology, sociology, and psychology. Indeed, these disciplines must provide the grounding for the major and for options within the major that are organized around certain integrative themes. For example, one option centering in child development should incorporate concepts from biology, psychology, sociology, and nutrition. Another in home management will embrace the subject matter and principles in textiles, economics, nutrition, and design. Students choosing these options should either enroll in relevant courses in the other departments involved or should take interdepartmental courses presented jointly by these departments and home economics and taught by professors holding joint appointments in both fields. Under no condition, however, should home economics independently offer these courses in established disciplines if they are offered elsewhere on campus.

For students planning to teach, the broad home economics curriculum should extend through all of the undergraduate years, with courses related to teacher preparation comprising only a portion of the fifth year. It is instructive to recall in this connection that over thirty years ago Effie Raitt was asking home economists if the time had come for a five-year program. Today, certainly as least in home economics education, the answer is yes. A similar master's program may be desirable for students entering Extension work, and eventually it may be necessary for those entering business.

At the master's level, home economics curricula should stress professional specialization, possibly through two principal tracks. One track would involve internship in a specific occupation through which home economics graduates could work either with practicing elementary and secondary teachers, with social workers in poverty programs, or with agricultural specialists in programs for underdeveloped countries. A second track at the master's level would involve the pursuit of an *applied* research project on some topic in home economics through an internship in the university itself. In either case the master's degree would be oriented directly to professional preparation.

At the doctoral level our study indicates that approximately ten universities have produced most of the personnel for college teaching and research in home economics. This pattern may change as more universities are urged to offer doctoral programs. In the years ahead, however, the profession and society as a whole will be better served if this advanced instruction continues to be concentrated in a limited number of institutions. There is no convincing evidence at present that for home economists to succeed outside of college teaching—for example, in business or industry—they will be required to earn the doctorate or, in the near future, for that matter, the master's degree. It is an established fact that offering a quality program in teaching or research at the doctoral level is one of the most costly undertakings any institution can become involved in. Moreover, a severely limited graduate program with inadequate staff and facilities may result in superficiality or provincial inquiries of little scholarly significance. Most important, however, it does not seem likely at present that the demand for doctorates in home economics will expand beyond the capacities of present institutions to produce them. *Hence, expansion in the number of doctoral programs can properly be resisted by administrators* unless there is a clearly unsatisifed need among the constituency and unless the substantial resources are available to meet the need at a suitable academic level. The claim is sometimes made that an institution can retain an excellent faculty only by offering doctoral work. This view overlooks the fact that other inducements such as salary, challenging undergraduate programs, and productive working conditions can be used to secure highly

128

qualified professors to man undergraduate and master's degree programs. The full report on this study contains a number of more detailed comments and recommendations about home economics curricula in land-grant colleges and state universities.

Extension services. There are, however, some observations about Extension services and research in home economics which should be placed before you at this time. Our inquiries revealed that the Extension programs in home economics serve groups that are composed disproportionately of whites, of people who dwell in rural areas, and of those who are not in the lowest financial stratum of society. These facts raise a basic question of educational and social policy in these days of social reform and the extension of educational opportunity. Should not the Extension programs be disproportionately serving exactly the opposite audience—the Negro, the city dweller, and the poor? A review of the facts in terms of the social conditions in the United States suggests that this shift in the orientation of Extension work seems patently essential and far overdue. This reorientation has been too long delayed in part by the domination of Cooperative Extension by a powerful network of vested interests at the national, state, and local levels determined to perpetuate existing agricultural structures, programs, and personnel. The future of home economics Extension will to a considerable degree depend on political decisions at these levels about Cooperative Extension at large. If its benefits are to be extended to the families of the city, the following major changes in its organization, administration, and methods will be necessary:

First, with the expansion and improvement of functions in the mass media, local community colleges, branch campuses of state universities, and adult education centers, the traditional methods of Cooperative Extension are becoming less and less adequate to fill the needs of our time. In the future these agencies should be able to provide much of the Extension service that in the past was the responsibility of the traveling county agent. They can also design and offer a much richer and more varied range of services.

Second, efforts now under way to integrate Cooperative Extension and its agrarian tradition with general university extension deserve the support of home economists and all others interested in raising the technical competence and the general understanding of our people. The activities of Cooperative Extension and general extension should ultimately be combined into one structure, with home economics Extension becoming an area of continuing education similar to the many other subject-matter fields now being made accessible to an evergrowing number of our citizens, particularly the adults. Because techniques and skills for working with urban dwellers must in some important ways be different from those employed in programs for farm families, the merger of these two types of services may have to proceed more slowly than is desirable; but the necessary expansion of urban Extension in home economics cannot be delayed much longer.

Finally, in each state the extension programs of all of the public colleges and universities, and where possible of privately supported institutions as well, should be coordinated by means of a state master plan to avoid useless duplication and to assure the most satisfactory distribution of services among all the citizens of the state. In some states, a state director of extension can administer this coordinated program, using staff members from all of the participating institutions, including state universities, state colleges, and community colleges. But regardless of the type of organization and administration adopted by any particular commonwealth, the legislature which must appropriate the funds for extension services and citizens generally ought to be able to feel that the needs of the people transcend institutional rivalry and empire building.

Research. Finally, the findings in this study confirm the view that, except in the area of nutrition, home economists in the land-grant colleges and universities as a group are not typically and continuously engaged in their own individual research projects; nor do they commonly become involved in cooperative interdisciplinary research. The dominance of research in nutrition is revealed in the fact that of 533 sponsored projects under way in departments of home economics at the time of the study, 42 percent were in food and nutrition. In less than 20 percent of all projects was the home economics staff collaborating with researchers in other departments; and in about half of these scattered interdepartmental research efforts, the other department involved was agriculture. The opportunities for interdisciplinary research involving home economics and the fruitful cooperation which has characterized other disciplines, particularly in the natural sciences, still remain to be developed. Currently, agricultural experiment stations or Hatch Act funds finance over 40 percent of the sponsored research projects in home economics. As valuable as this assistance is, government and industry must provide additional funds which will enable home economics to expand its investigations and extend them increasingly into areas of research not directly related to agriculture.

John Dewey once wrote, "There is no more a special independent science of education than there is of bridge-building." This statement obviously applies with equal force and relevance to home economics. Home economics, to be sure, can and ought to contribute its own unique orientation or angle of vision to research involving the family and home life; but, to assure that the investigations undertaken possess both substance and broad significance, it is essential that working relationships be established with productive scholars in other disciplines. It should not be necessary to defend this proposal. There is abundant evidence to show that the most fruitful new ideas in many other fields of knowledge, and their application to human problems, often come from individuals who are working on projects which border on fields other than their own specialty and who view problems from a "marginal" perspective. Many of these outside explorers have brought to their research a novel orientation which has produced the most arresting innovative ideas and procedures. The need for scholars in other disciplines in the arts and sciences to collaborate in home economics research is suggested by the fact that three out of every four professors of home economics in the land-grant colleges and state universities have never held any position outside of home economics. Thus, they tend to think in terms of established subject matter, procedures, and traditions within the field and overlook the opportunities which lie concealed in unexplored adjacent terrain.

As in the case of education for the doctorate, a few land-grant colleges and state universities dominate research in home economics. The findings in this study show that among 49 of the land-grant colleges 7 institutions account for 45 percent of the active research projects. In contrast to an earlier recommendation that doctoral programs be limited to a few well-qualified institutions, it is recommended that applied research programs in home economics be dispersed over a wider number of institutions in order to permit faculty members at these institutions to participate in the intellectually invigorating pursuit of new knowledge and to provide internships in applied research enterprises for students working for the master's degree.

Conclusion

In conclusion, to expand the three functions of teaching, Extension, and research that have been the subject of these recommendations may require a reorganization of home economics programs within the state universities and land-grant colleges. For example, to assure widespread cooperation in interdisciplinary research and teaching, it may be necessary to consider structural reorganization in the university so that schools or departments of home economics can be placed in closer relationships with other units. Newly created colleges of human resources or human development at several universities illustrate the types of such possible arrangements in which home economics is coordinated with the social sciences to assure continuous dialogue between the relevant professional groups and teaching and research effort in cooperation with the basic disciplines. At other institutions, to facilitate the preparation of skilled professional practitioners able to work in professional teams, home economics could become a unit in a College of Applied Arts and Sciences organically connected with other units in education, journalism, and business. In still other institutions it may be necessary for the time to maintain a separate and autonomous unit in home economics. With respect to organization and administration, however, one fact stands out in this study: the programs of home economics now under the jurisdiction of schools of agriculture should be given greater autonomy and freedom in establishing relationships with a wide range of disciplines in the liberal arts colleges and in the professional and graduate schools. Only under such an administrative and structural reorganization will home economics be able to reorient itself away from its traditional limited purposes toward the broader educational and social needs of a culture which continues to change swiftly from the conditions of American life exisiting when home economics came into being.

There is no single realignment which will automatically produce the most effective structure. Nor will a gradual evolutionary process produce the desired changes. The initiative and encouragement of university presidents and deans, representing the interests of the total institution and its constituency, will be required as well as support from outside the universities. One such extramural agency is the federal government. Through the years, the organization and scope of home economics as a college subject have been greatly influenced by federal legislation—in particular, the Hatch Act of 1887, the Smith-Lever Act of 1914, and the Smith-Hughes Act of 1917. The future course of home economics in the land-grant colleges and state universities will be affected no less profoundly by the character and purposes of federal legislation and support.

Existing federal and state legislation and agreements that undergird home economics education, Extension, and research in the land-grant colleges do not provide enough latitude or stimulation to enable home economics to meet the changing needs of the time. This is particularly true of the statutes and regulations governing the Cooperative Extension Service. A thoroughgoing review of the adequacy of these legislative acts and agreements should be launched at once at the highest levels of government to assure that home economics is enabled and, indeed, required to redesign its programs and services to meet the needs of American society which have emerged during the past 50 years. Particular attention in this review should be given to the confining relationships now existing between county government and agrarian interests. Such a review will unquestionably show that large additional federal support is urgently required to allow home economics to fulfill its potentially rich variety of services needed to help raise the conditions of life among the urban poor in America and impoverished throughout the world.

Home economics was born at a time when the United States economy was oriented to agriculture and when its most direct beneficiaries were farm families. No one who knows the history of its immeasurable contributions to the rural areas would suggest that they should now be neglected or bypassed. But today this rural orientation is disturbing to those who wish to bring the teaching, research, and Extension services of home economics into broader contact with the whole of American society. Among the land-grant institutions in the various states and regions the ties of home economics with both agricultural and city life will properly vary because of differences in population concentration, vocations, and the conditions of life generally. But home economics must view American society as a whole and respond to the needs of the cities, the countries abroad, and our overarching economic requirements as well as the needs of rural society. If it fails to keep abreast of these demands it will lose much of its support and the gratitude of a society to which it has richly contributed. More importantly, the functions and services it fails to provide will be assumed by other agencies. With federal support, with the encouragement of the administrators responsible for the total institutional program, and with the imaginative planning of leaders within the field, there is no reason why home economists cannot in the future benefit the families of generations yet to come at home and abroad as fully as they have enriched the lives of countless Americans in the days which have passed. It is our devout hope that this study may be helpful in the achievement of this worthy goal.

16

New Challenges for Home Economics Educators

Mary Lee Hurt and Margaret Alexander
U.S. Department of Health, Education, and Welfare

On October 16, 1968, the 90th Congress passed Public Law 90-576 to amend the Vocational Education Act of 1963. The authors of this article, in their positions in the U.S. Office of Education, have been actively involved in planning the implementation of Part F of Title I, entitled "Consumer and Homemaking Education." They present here challenges that the legislation offers home economics educators.

The Vocational Education Amendments of 1968 have presented home economics educators with one of the greatest challenges since the passage of the first federal legislation for the support of vocational education. A separate section of this legislation, Part F of Title I, authorizes allotments of funds on a matching basis to states for "Consumer and Homemaking Education." At least one-third of the funds made available under this section are to be used for programs in depressed areas or areas of high unemployment (1).

A contributing factor to the passage of Part F as a distinct section was the fact that members of Congress recognized what home economics programs in schools can offer individuals and families to help them cope with the complex problems of today's world. They were sensitive to the contributions that can be made to families, particularly those in the inner cities and rural areas who are beset with the problems of poverty. Selected statements of members of Congress, excerpted from the hearings and reports, show this support.

The Committee on Education and Labor, House of Representatives, strongly supported a separate authorization for homemaking programs that "protects the continuance of a program which has been highly successful in training young women to be successful wives and mothers of the future . . . The committee hopes that homemaking teachers and supervisors across the nation will pick up the challenge of today's changing society by making the new set-aside for programs in economically depressed areas a success." A number of senators also spoke out in support of a separate authorization. Senator Yarborough of Texas expressed his support in this way: "This section will for the first time, bring homemaking education into the legislative picture in a formal manner—being specifically set forth and given its own place in the sun. . . . Running a home in the 20th Century is no easy task. . ."

Home economics education programs can make significant contributions in helping to meet varying needs of families, according to Senator Sparkman of Alabama. He spoke in support of the legislation by saying: "Think of the potential impact that a good basic education in home economics can have on the improvement of the standard of living and basic happiness of every American family. . . . We have only begun to scratch the surface in providing home economics for the disadvantaged and low-income families. There are also great needs among the physically and mentally handicapped. Special programs are also needed for newly established households." Representative Pucinski of Illinois worked for continued legislative support for home economics education because he could see that programs could be expanded to make a significant contribution by preparing women for the dual role of homemaker and wage earner. In the hearings he voiced his support with this statement: ". . . it would seem to me that we ought to give home economics a high priority. . . . I think that we ought to teach the young woman not only something about her responsibilities as a mother and a homemaker, but also prepare her for the eventuality that she will become one of the 50 percent of mothers who are going to have to go [out] and earn a living for her family."

Requirements of the Legislation

"Consumer and homemaking education" is defined in the "Regulations for State Plan Programs" (2), which states must meet to qualify for funding under the provisions of Part F of the Vocational Education Amendments of 1968, as "education designed to help individuals and families improve home environments and the quality of personal and family life . . . [it] includes instruction in food and nutrition, child development, clothing, housing, family relations, and management of resources with emphasis on selection, use, and care of goods and services, budgeting, and other consumer responsibilities."

Funds allotted to the states for the purpose of Part F of the Amendments may be used for consumer and homemaking programs and for ancillary services and activities to assure quality in these programs. The following requirements must be met for a program to receive approval (3):

(a) The program will encourage greater consideration of the social and cultural conditions and needs, especially in economically depressed areas;

(b) The program will encourage preparation for professional leadership in home economics and consumer education;

(c) The program will be designed for youth and adults who have entered or are preparing to enter the work of the home;

(d) The program will be designed to prepare such youth and adults for the role of homemaker or to contribute to their employability in the dual role of homemaker and wage earner; and

(e) The program will include consumer education as an integral part thereof.

Challenges for Program Planning

The requirements of the new legislation offer specific challenges to home economics educators to develop programs which will make a real difference in the quality of living of individuals and families today. Programs should differ to a greater extent than ever before if they are planned with due consideration of the social and cultural differences unique to each community. The content of programs will vary to reflect the legislative mandates. Five of the major challenges to program planning are discussed.

Encourage home economics to give greater consideration to social and cultural conditions and needs, especially in depressed areas. The word "greater" would seem to indicate that home economics is already giving attention to this provision. The challenge is to do more. It is true that home economics teachers have always tried to relate curriculum to the needs of individuals and families in the community being served. Communities are changing, and home economics education programs must change too. For example, in the inner city, home economics teachers can help both in-school youth and also adults who have recently moved to the city from rural areas, to acquire new patterns of living for coping with an entirely new environment. In rural depressed areas, home economics curricula can be adapted to the particular backgrounds of the students and their families. Teachers can help students apply in their homes what they have learned in class, and teachers can offer help and counsel to their students' mothers as requested. Home economics curricula in schools in suburban and affluent communities should be examined as well as those in depressed areas to make sure that objectives and learning experiences are relevant to the lives of the students. Ethnic and cultural characteristics of families in the community, levels of income, types of housing, average age of marriages, the extent to which mothers with children work outside the home, and community services available to children and families, are some of the factors to be considered by home economics teachers as curricula are planned "to give greater consideration to social and cultural conditions and needs."

Encourage preparation for professional leadership. Jobs on the paraprofessional level are expanding as society requests more services for children and elderly people, and as families demand more meals away from home and additional housekeeping and clothing care services. Professional home economists continue to be in short supply in relation to the demands for the traditional type of positions such as in teaching, Extension, business, and institution management, and for the many new positions emerging in the health, welfare, and community development fields.

This challenge means that additional efforts need to be made to provide opportunities for students to find out about the wide range of occupational and career possibilities available in home economics and to encourage those with appropriate interests and aptitudes to plan a career in the field. Guidance counselors can be provided with materials and information they may use when counseling students. The program of the Future Homemakers of America has always stressed careers in home economics, and opportunities are provided for members to become acquainted with individuals in their work on both the paraprofessional and professional levels. These opportunities can be expanded.

Design programs to prepare youth and adults for the role of homemaker or to contribute to their employability in the dual role of homemaker and wage earner. Traditionally the main purpose of home economics education has been to prepare homemakers. Congress in its new legislation indicates that this purpose should continue to be served, but it presents us with an additional challenge: we also should prepare youth and adults to assume the "dual role" of managing home and family responsibilities and a job outside the home.

"Contributing to employability" means helping youth and adults acquire personal qualities needed for success on the job. Some of these are punctuality, responsibility, trustworthiness, ability to work with others, and acceptable appearance. For women, especially those with families, this also means the ability to manage home and family responsiblities so that they can be at work regularly and on time and be free from concern during employment. The area of management as part of home economics programs needs special emphasis. This includes the study of management principles relating to decision-making, goals, values, standards, and use of various resources; money management and consumer education; application of nutrition principles in providing food for the physical well-being of individuals of different ages; and acquisition of adequate housing and its care. Roles of family members and how they will change when mother works outside the home need to be studied.

A curriculum package of helpful suggestions for preparing students for the dual role of homemaker and wage earner was developed and tested by Hughes (4). Topics for which teaching suggestions were developed are: why women work outside the home, deciding to work, costs of employment, provisions for care of children, and money management.

It is recognized that socioeconomically deprived youth usually need much help with personal problems and with how to get and keep a job; most will be compelled to carry the dual role later in life. Lowe, Nelson, and Dalrymple (5), three researchers in home economics education, have developed curriculum materials to test some new approaches for home economics courses for disadvantaged inner city youth who are preparing to assume the role of homemaker-wage earner. Additional research and demonstration programs like this study are needed. The materials developed in the project have been tested in inner city schools in Indiana, Ohio, New York, and Connecticut. The first several units of one of the courses developed are grouped under "Skills for Living," and students are helped to understand themselves and to build a positive self-concept. The second series of units under "Introduction to Skills in Food Service" prepares students for getting a part-time food service job. Each student is helped to secure work of this type, and problems on the job form the basis for classwork. For the first time many of these students are earning money and deciding how to spend their earnings to meet their many needs. This makes for stimulating class discussions. The last few units in the course, grouped under "Skills for Homemaking and the Dual Role," deal with managing the responsibilities of homemakers who are employed outside the home. Students continue on their part-time jobs throughout the year, and the home economics teachers supervise and help them as needed.

Make consumer education an integral part of the program. Consumer education has always been included in the home economics curriculum of the schools, but sometimes it has been so integrated that neither teachers nor students recognized it as consumer education. To meet the demands of today, consumer education must be expanded in scope and made visible as part of home economics education programs for both in-school youth and adults. Units on consumer education need to be expanded as a part of comprehensive home economics courses as well as being made available as separate course offerings. The chief concern of consumer education, as a part of home economics education for both youth and adults, is the wise use of the income and other resources in feeding, clothing, and housing the individual and family; rearing children; and maintaining satisfying human relations. Consumer decisions should be made in the context of goals for improving home environment and the quality of family life. Money is a personal and family resource which may be used as a tool in achieving a satisfactory life. The challenge is to reach as many individuals as possible through consumer education. To expand the opportunities for students to enroll in consumer education, some courses can be developed and taught by a team of teachers from different subject areas.

Provide ancillary services to insure quality in programs. Changes in home economics programs in the schools also require changes in pre-service teacher education programs and expansion of in-service help for teachers. New or revised curriculum and instructional materials are needed to effect changes in programs. Ancillary services such as these, plus research, program evaluation, demonstration and experimental programs, provision for equipment, and state administration and leadership, may be supported under the provisions of the new legislation in order to assure quality in all programs. Home economics education leaders are being challenged to develop long-range and yearly state plans for programs to be offered and for the ancillary services to undergird these programs in their states.

Expansion and Redirection of Programs

When Congress passed Part F of the 1968 Vocational Education Amendments supporting consumer and homemaking education, it offered both challenges and opportunities to reevaluate present programs to be sure that they are really making differences in the lives of the youth and adults who enroll. Experimenting with differently organized programs and trying new approaches and ways of reaching different groups of people, may result in reaching more girls and boys and women and men with the type of consumer and homemaking education geared to their different environments.

• In some schools comprehensive courses on the junior high level, including the ninth grade, provide some students with a new image of family life and develop attitudes and abilities basic to personal development and later to the establishment of their own homes. Semester offerings open to 10th, 11th, and 12th graders in subject-matter areas such as child development, family relations, food and nutrition, textiles and clothing, housing and furnishings, and consumer education and home management may meet additional needs of students and offer a selection for those with special interests. A comprehensive course for seniors offered in some schools meets the needs of those who have not been able to schedule home economics courses earlier during high school. Family living courses for junior and senior students (boys and girls), including the study of personal and family relationships, child development, consumer education, management, and nutrition, which are felt to be important aspects of general education today, may meet the needs of many students. In some schools separate classes for boys may be particularly helpful. This might be true in schools in depressed areas where boys need much help with personal development as well as experiences which will help them assume their expected roles as workers and heads of families. A man-woman team of teachers would be especially helpful in working with boys having such needs.

• In schools where there is flexible scheduling and where individualized instructional experiences are offered, students may select the learning modules of most interest and fit them into their individual schedules whenever possible.

• In some states home economics departments in technical institutes or junior and/or community colleges offer courses in child development and family life, consumer education and management, and food and nutrition, as well as courses that prepare for occupations utilizing home economics knowledge and skills. Home economics teachers need to work with their colleagues in other vocational education services to plan ways to include some education for family responsibilities in the programs of all vocational education students.

New approaches and new relationships are being established between the home economics departments in the schools and agencies and organizations in the community, particularly to reach adults and families in depressed areas.

• Cooperative programs with the Public Housing Authority have existed in a number of communities for several years, and these are expanding. Classroom space is provided by the Public Housing Authority; the teachers' salaries and instructional supplies are supported from local school, state, and federal vocational education funds. Teachers are assigned to certain public housing centers; they offer classes for homemakers throughout the day or evening and also give individual help to homemakers whenever needed. Housekeeping clinics are held with the help of the management of housing developments. In a number of housing projects, children's centers are equipped and supervised so that mothers may attend classes and also participate in parent study groups. Day care centers have been set up in a number of housing centers for children of working mothers. Many families have learned to manage their resources through these programs; some have been able to make down payments on homes, and all have improved the quality of home life.

• Providing an educational component in homemaking for the welfare program in the community is a way of supplementing the help provided for some families. In other communities educational programs are being coordinated with public health food and nutrition services. Mothers of children in those school programs receiving support under the provisions of Title I, Elementary and Secondary Education Act of 1965, would be a captive group for adult education classes, especially in nutrition and consumer education.

• In some communities the National Alliance of Businessmen, or other groups offering manpower training programs, may need assistance from homemaking teachers in teaching the participants or their wives in job-training programs, money management, personal grooming, health, and human relationships. Basic education and homemaking teachers are cooperating in developing lessons which will not only help individuals to learn to read but also give help in consumer education, nutrition, and family life.

140

• Mobile classrooms with instructors and teaching materials are being set up for some inner city areas.

• In communities in some states, coordinated programs have been developed with the home economics Extension service to avoid overlaps and to help strengthen total community programs.

Local advisory committees and personal contacts with local agencies can help supervisors and teachers identify opportunities where and when the school may offer educational programs in consumer and homemaking education to groups who may profit from these programs. Adult education programs in home economics today must reach out into the neighborhoods where the people are and help to provide in many cases an educational component as a part of ongoing community programs.

Let's Not Forget—Two Purposes of Vocational Home Economics Programs

Consumer and homemaking education programs are being expanded and redirected under the provisions of Part F of the 1968 Amendments to Vocational Education. But increased opportunities for programs which prepare for gainful occupations utilizing home economics knowledge and skills are available under the support for all vocational programs. Part B of the 1968 Amendments provides for increased grants to states to expand vocational education programs for persons of all ages in all communities of the states who desire and need such training. With the increased need for trained personnel for group care of children, for services for elderly people, for household and institutional housekeeping services, and for food and clothing services, home economics educators have another big challenge and responsibility ahead, namely, the preparation of paraprofessionals in the field of home economics. As the two aspects of home economics education programs—consumer and homemaking and occupational preparation—continue to expand and gain depth, it is essential to maintain them as parts of a total program in home economics education. As new knowledge and skills are discovered, the big challenge to home economists is to find ways to put this knowledge and these skills to work in helping people help themselves in attaining richer, more satisfying lives as members of families and also, for some, as workers in occupations which serve the needs of individuals and families.

References

1. Public Law 90-576, October 16, 1968. *Vocational Education Amendments of 1968,* "Title I, Part F," p. 22.

2. Bureau of Adult, Vocational, and Library Programs, U.S. Department of Health, Education, and Welfare. *Regulations for State Plan Programs, Vocational Education Amendments of 1968.* Washington, D.C., April 1969, p. 10. (Material for *administrative use only.*)

3. *Ibid.,* pp. 99-100.

4. Hughes, R. B. Preparation for a dual role. *J. Home Econ.,* Vol. 61, No. 5 (May 1969), pp. 350-358.

5. Lowe, P. K., Nelson, H. Y., and Dalrymple, J. "The Efficacy of Home Economics Courses Designed to Prepare Disadvantaged Pupils for Their Homemaker-Family Member Role and the Dual Roles of Homemaker and Wage Earner," a three-part study funded under the provisions of Sec. 4(c) of the Vocational Education Act of 1963, to be completed October 1970.

PART FOUR

Priorities for the 70's
1970 - 1979

Home Economics works through the family to effect an optimum balance between people and their environments. Home Economics accepts the challenge of helping people to adjust to change and to shape the future.

The core of Home Economics is the family ecosystem. It is the study of the reciprocal relations of family to its natural and man-made environments, the effect of these singly or in unison as they shape the internal functioning of families, and the interplays between the family and other social institutions and the physical environment.

NEW DIRECTIONS II
Bivens et al - 1975

17

The Family
As An Ecosystem

Nancy C. Hook & Beatrice Paolucci
Michigan State University

This article suggests a historical perspective of the profession's long-held view of the family as a life support system and presents some approaches for helping students to understand the interdependencies of man with man and with his environment.

The quality of man's life and the prospects for his continued survival within a limited environmental setting are today receiving national and international attention. Over time home economists, along with other professionals, have been concerned with developing and promoting social, economic, and technological innovations which at one level have enhanced man's quality of life but which at another level may have unwittingly limited the potential for life. The rapid depletion of essential resources and the necessity to maintain man's humanness has forced us to reconsider the interdependence of man and his environment.

Home economics was defined by the participants of the Lake Placid Conferences as the study:

. . . of the laws, conditions, principles and ideals which are concerned on the one hand with man's immediate physical environment and on the other hand with his nature as a social being, and is the study specially of the relation between those two factors (1).

As viewed today, these pioneers were defining an ecological framework. They considered and discarded the term ecology based on the fact that "botanists had already appropriated this word and established its use in their science" (2). Historically, Ernest Hacckel in an effort to formulate a logical scheme in the zoological sciences coined the word "ecology" (occology) around the 1870's to emphasize "the fact that the structure and behavior of organisms are significantly affected by their living together with other organisms of the same and other species and by their habitat" (3). Ecology is derived from the Greek word *oikos*—a house or place in which to live. From this same root word come the terms *economy* and *economics*. In the early 20's Robert E. Park and Ernest W. Burgess adopted the use of "human ecology" within the field of sociology. Generally ecology is the study of the relation of organisms or groups of organisms to their environment.

In retrospect, ecology might have been a suitable choice of name for the area of study now known as home economics, for the term forces one to emphasize the interdependent relationship between man and his environment. In the field of home economics, this interdependent relationship basically focuses on the home as a life support system for family members; that is, provision of both physical and social nurturance.

This approach of viewing the home and/or family as an ecosystem provides a framework to assist home economists in meeting the challenge of man's survival. What constitutes the study of the home as an ecosystem?

> Ecologists use the term ecosystem to refer to a community together with its habitat. An ecosystem, then, is an aggregation of associated species of plants and animals, together with the physical features of their habitat. Ecosystems . . . can be of any size or ecologic rank. Thus, a drop of pond water together with the organisms that live therein constitutes a small ecosystem. At the extreme, the whole earth and all its plant and animal inhabitants together constitute a world ecosystem. The concept of ecosystem emphasizes the interrelations between the group of organisms that form a community, and . . . its environment (4).

At the 1908 Lake Placid Conference (5), home was defined as "the place of shelter and nurture for the children and for those personal qualities of self-sacrifice for others for the gaining of strength to meet the world. . . ." Interpretation of this definition has sometimes become a limiting stereotype of one-family dwellings with an overemphasis on the material aspects. Home economists have tended to take a unifocal view of both the environment (that is, food, clothing, and shelter) and the family (its relationships and development of individuals). They have neglected to look at the family as an interdependent life support system.

The family as a life support system is dependent upon the natural environment for physical sustenance and upon the social organizations which are related to man's humanness and give quality and meaning to life. Home economists for some time have emphasized the social-emotional environment. It is necessary for the field (as it focuses on the family) to link both the natural environment and the social environment. Therein lie its uniqueness and strength.

Understanding and accepting the consequences of this interdependence is critical to man's survival. A noted ecologist, John Cantlon (6), recently stated:

> The Congress should undertake to expedite eliminating the serious lack of environmental understanding in the public educated citizenry of the country. . . .

One example of a place to start would be to encourage the home economics curricula in the United States to adopt as a curricular focal point "the home as an ecosystem." Learning to think of each household as a system of inputs and losses of energy and materials would provide a means of relating to the larger urban and rural ecosystems. It would be rather simple to quantify the coupling of each individual in a systems way to his requirements from air, water, and food sheds, from fuel and other resources; as well as coupling his waste outputs to these regional sheds and man's larger ecosystems. Learning how these systems operate and where he fits in the picture may help alleviate some feelings of alienation between the individual and various components of his environment. Learning what affects the health of the ecosystems that sustain and inspire him may make him a better informed voting citizen.

The primary question is: What constitutes the study of the family as an ecosystem?

We define family as a corporate unit of interacting and interdependent personalities who have a common theme and goals, have a commitment over time, and share resources and living space. Hawley (7) defined the family as:

A relatively small association of individuals, differing in age and sex, who, as a result of their close physical association in a common residence and their mutually sustaining activities, form a distinguishable entity or unit within a larger aggregate.

These definitions are seen as mutually compatible.

The writers of this paper recommend the blending of perspectives of human ecology as traditionally developed by sociologists and biologists. The approach is ecological: a search for *understanding* and *controlling* the mutually sustaining relationships that couple man with his environment.

An Approach for Home Economics

A single profession can bring knowledge to bear on only a limited part of the environment; hence, home economists generally define their sphere of concern as the *family* and that part of the near environment that impinges directly upon the family and is subject to manipulation by the family. Home economists attend to the *interaction* of man as a total being and his near environment, *especially as this interaction is managed by the family.*

The approach using concepts developed by sociology is that of Duncan's (8) ecological complex or POET model—population, organization, environment, and technology. How does this complex relate to the way home economists can view the family as an ecosystem?

Population. According to Duncan, population refers to a concrete population of human organisms more or less circumscribed territorially. This population aggregate has unit character and significant properties which differ from the properties of its component elements. Family may be viewed as the population. The family is a corporate unit with symbiotic relationships. The position of this paper views the family as a population aggregate or system that is, a corporate unit which is circumscribed territorially within a household and which has some unit character differing from the characteristics of its individual members such as its theme or value system and cyclic development.

Organization. Organization arises from sustenance-producing activities. It is a property of the population aggregate, is indispensable to the maintenance of collective life, and must be adapted to the conditions confronting a population. Organization is a communication and control system which functions to maintain unity and to accomplish work. This is a major concept of family managerial behavior. The assumptions of organization made by Duncan (8) come close to those of the family management specialist (9, 10, 11). Examination of information flows in the ecosystem is as pertinent as examination of energy flows. According to Duncan ". . . information serves to control" is one function of management (12). This is related to the decision-making function of the family and is fundamental to the ecological approach. In addition to the traditional food, clothing, and shelter arenas of family decision-making to which home economists have attended, attention must now be focused on value considerations which include controlling population and technology for the ultimate benefit of mankind.

Environment. In a very general sense, environment can be defined as whatever is external to and potentially or actually influential on a phenomenon (a system, an organism, an object). The environment is seen as providing resources potentially useful for the maintenance of life. The population acts upon the environment and the environment acts upon the population. This adjustment is a continuing dynamic process.

Components of the environment with which the family interacts and with which it is interdependent may be considered as: the physical and biological environment, which includes land, water, air, space, the solar system, plants and animals, sources of food and energy. The social environment includes the social institutions of society: the kinship, religious, political, economic, productive, recreative; and the symbolic and ideological systems. Within this total environment can be superimposed three human systems: (1) the biophysical—physiological and metabolic processes, the organic life cycle; (2) the psychosocial—interpersonal relationships expressed by individual and collective patterns of behavior; and (3) the technological—materials, tools, and techniques (13).

The technological subsystem includes parts of both the physical and the social environments; for example, a dishwasher utilizes water from the physical environment, which is controlled through the social environment. The availability of a pure water supply depends upon elaborate social organizations which provide service to homes in this country, in addition to the technological developments which have led to the construction of dams, purification systems, and the like.

Man, being both biophysical and psychosocial, serves as a connecting and controlling link between these systems. The family is seen as both an environment for the individual and as existing in a larger physical and biological environment and social environment. The family exists within only part of the total environment; there are spatial and temporal dimensions which need to be considered. This is especially true in a post-industrial society.

Technology. This has been included within the environment in the preceding discussion. Technology refers to a set of techniques employed by a population to gain sustenance from its environment and to facilitate the organization of sustenance-producing activity. In effect, technology has the potential for redefining the environment.

A simple approach to viewing the family as an ecosystem is to consider energy flows. Adams (14) has listed two major ways in which energy relates to human organizations: (1) an organization is an ordering of energy and (2) human organizations are converters of energy. Examination of this aspect requires knowledge of biological ecology and an understanding of caloric intake, coupled with the energy requirements necessary for carrying out social and economic functions of household and family activity and work patterns.

One consideration might be the material inputs that come into the family, such as purchases from the grocery. Computations could be determined of the energy inputs from food, paper, detergents, plastics, cloth, cosmetics, drugs, and other commodities, in addition to energy sources such as electricity, heat, and labor, which are essential in converting matter for consumption. Balancing against these energy inputs would be computations of family activity and work pattern outputs. It also is important to realize the essentiality of overall balance, recognizing that costs ensue from energy and material losses. For example, the material inputs from the grocery result in human and nonhuman waste which contributes to the pollution problem. Waste that is recycled is not a problem; that which is not recycled mars the landscapes and pollutes the environment. Much of this recycling is now left to chance. In the future, families will need to recognize their role in maintaining an energy balance and living in harmony with nature.

These approaches do not have mutually exclusive variables; it is readily observable that there is overlap. The approaches may be useful in helping students understand interdependencies of man with man and with his environment. Interdependencies of man with man could be seen as the reciprocal effects of individuals within a family and reciprocal effects of families with other families, and the effects of both on the environment.

Rapid scientific and technological developments have pushed scientists to consider the alternatives of present action in terms of their long-range consequences. Since the Industrial Revolution, the ecosystem has included the machines devised by man, their products and their incalculable capacity to alter the natural balances.

There is no longer an "away." One person's trash basket is another's living space . . . there are not *consumers*—only users. The user employs the product, sometimes changes it in form, but does not consume it—he just discards it. Discard creates residues that pollute at an increasing cost to the consumer and to his community (15).

A solution to these problems requires welding together the physical, biological, and social sciences to help define and achieve an environment of a quality satisfactory to human well-being and aspiration. As Cain (16) stated, "The only true synthesis would be that which recognizes the real nature of human ecosystems, a recognition of all the significant relationships between man and environment." The centrality of this approach to man's survival and the role for home economics was pointed out by Cantlon (6). The charge and challenge are clear.

References

1. *Lake Placid Conference on Home Economics. Proceedings of Conferences 1 to 10, 1899-1908*. Washington, D.C.: American Home Economics Association. Proceedings of the fourth annual conference, 1902, pp. 70-71.

2. *Lake Placid Conference on Home Economics. Proceedings of Conferences 1 to 10, 1899-1908*. Washington, D.C.: American Home Economics Association. Proceedings of the sixth annual conference, 1904, p. 63.

3. Wirth, L. Human Ecology. In *Studies in Human Ecology*, G. A. Theodorson (Editor). New York: Harper & Row, Publishers, 1961, p. 71.

4. Dice, L. R. *Man's Nature and Nature's Man*. Ann Arbor: University of Michigan Press, 1955, p. 2.

5. *Lake Placid Conference on Home Economics. Proceedings of Conferences 1 to 10, 1899-1908*. Washington, D.C.: American Home Economics Association. Proceedings of the tenth annual conference, 1908, p. 22.

6. Cantlon, J. In *Colloquium to Discuss a National Policy for the Environment*. Joint hearing before Senate Committee on Interior and Insular Affairs and House Committee on Science and Astronautics, 90th Cong., 2nd Sess., 1968, pp. 153-154.

7. Hawley, A. H. *Human Ecology*. New York: The Ronald Press Company, 1950, p. 211.

8. Duncan, O. D. Human Ecology and Population Studies. In *The Study of Population*, P. Hauser and O. D. Duncan (Editors). Chicago: University of Chicago Press, 1959, pp. 678-716.

9. Paolucci, B. Contributions of a framework of home management to the teaching of family relationships. *J. Marriage & the Family*, Vol. 28 (1966), pp. 338-342.

10. Schlater, J. D. The management process and its core concepts. *J. Home Econ.*, Vol. 59, No. 2 (Feb. 1967), pp. 93-98.

11. Steidl, R. E. An Ecological Approach to the Study of Family Managerial Behavior. Speech at conference on The Family: Focus on Management, Pennsylvania State University, June 30, 1969.

12. Duncan, O. D. Social Organization and the Ecosystem. In *Handbook of Modern Sociology*, R. E. L. Faris (Editor). Chicago: Rand McNally & Company, 1964, p. 41.

13. McHale, J. Global ecology: Toward the planetary society. *Am. Behavioral Scientist*, Vol. 11, No. 6 (1968), p. 30.

14. Adams, R. N. Energy Analysis of Social Organization. Unpublished paper, Michigan State University, Nov. 1959.

15. *Waste Management and Control*. National Academy of Sciences. National Research Council Publication 1400, 1966, pp. 3, 5.

16. Cain, S. A. Can Ecology Provide the Basis for Synthesis Among the Social Science? In *Social Sciences and the Environment*, M. E. Garnsey and J. R. Hibbs (Editors). Boulder: University of Colorado Press, 1967, p. 40.

18

Vocational Home Economics Present and Future

Mary Lee Hurt
Education Program Specialist, U.S. Office of Education

How relevant is vocational home economics to today's societal needs?

• In Alabama, clothing service workers train to establish businesses of their own.

• In Arkansas, high school girls (and boys) prepare for the dual role of homemaker-wage earner.

• In California, senior girls and boys discuss purposes of families, values, and decisionmaking.

• In Georgia, young men and women in postsecondary vocational schools study consumer and family life skills.

• In Illinois, food service workers and supervisors prepare for jobs.

• In Iowa, Future Homemakers of America "adopt" senior citizens.

• In Kentucky, day care operators upgrade their child care and child development skills.

• In Minnesota, pregnant teenage girls continue schooling until graduation through the work of the home economics teachers.

• In Montana, Indian women help teach homemaking to Indian girls.

• In New Mexico, opportunities to work with children keep Spanish-American eighth grade girls in school.

• In Ohio, vocational home economics educators provide the leadership for consumer education programs for pupils from kindergarten through twelfth grade.

• In Oregon, a mobile unit with a teacher and aides takes home economics instruction to the inner city and to a migrant camp.

- In Pennsylvania, middle-school girls and boys learn to value children and to help at home.

- In Tennessee, programs provide training for homemaker-home health aides.

- In Texas, cooperative supervised work experiences in social agencies, business, and industry prepare youth for home economics occupations.

- In Washington State, the Food Education and Service Training (FEAST) program keeps disadvantaged youth in school. In this state, too, thousands of parents enroll in parent education classes and their children in cooperative nursery schools.

Variations to Meet Community Needs

These examples, typical of those in most states, suggest the wide range of vocational home economics programs available throughout the nation's schools. Programs vary to meet the needs of individuals and families but are also dependent on the resources available and support from local administration and members of the community. Local leadership usually dictates the amount of creativity.

Large school districts may offer extensive programs comprised of consumer and homemaking education, and preparation for home economics occupations. The consumer and homemaking education aspect provides the foundation for occupational programs. It also contributes to the development of qualities that help youth become employable and, in addition, offers preparation for the dual role of homemaker and wage earner. Occupational training programs develop the understandings, abilities, and skills in a particular area of home economics to the point that a student acquires a salable skill needed in the labor market.

Small school districts may offer only consumer and homemaking education and possibly training for one occupational area. Area vocational schools may offer additional opportunities for occupational preparation.

Career education is an added dimension of educational programs at the present time and one to which home economics is making a significant contribution. The goal of the career education program is to insure that all children and youth leave school with skills sufficient to obtain employment, pursue further career training, or enter higher levels of education. Its fundamental concept is that "all educational experiences—curriculum, instruction, and counseling—should be geared to preparation for economic independence, personal fulfillment, and an appreciation for the dignity of work" (6).

Through revised curriculums in the elementary school, children, it is hoped, will relate what they learn to the varied ways by which adults earn a living. As they continue through middle or junior high school the young will become increasingly oriented to the world of work and grow more and more aware of their own interests and talents. They will begin to explore several specific clusters of careers that interest them. In early high school they will be provided further exploratory experiences and start to narrow their career interests to perhaps two or three related clusters. By the time students have reached the upper grades of high school it is hoped that at least 80 percent of all youth, excepting those who definitely are capable of preparing for the professions, will then concentrate on a cluster of occupations and gain sufficient skill in a special occupation to qualify for a job. Their programs will be planned, however, so that they may always change to a related occupation and continue their education if their first choice does not seem to be suitable or if additional opportunities for further education are available.

Vocational home economics can contribute to career education at all levels.

Middle schools and junior high schools, including various combinations of grades 5 through 8, provide an opportunity to help students become acquainted with many styles of family life—with factors that contribute to family stability and with the multiple roles that some family members must assume. Here girls and boys in homemaking learn how to help with some tasks, care for children, help with the shopping for self and family, get along with friends and family, and acquire basic qualities that later contribute to employability. Pupils learn about the various occupations and professions open in home economics.

In some schools, particularly those in disadvantaged areas, the homemaking teachers work closely with the families of the girls and boys to interpret the school's aims for the children and to seek the parents' counsel in what to teach that will prove most helpful. In some cases the school offers adult classes in consumer and homemaking education for the parents in homes or neighborhood centers. Many pupils are being kept in school because of the dedicated interest and efforts of these teachers.

The early years of secondary school provide opportunities to reach many students with comprehensive courses in consumer and homemaking education. Included are units in child development, personal-family relationships, consumer education, nutrition and family meal management, clothing and textiles, home furnishings, and care of the home.

Schools in some states offer 1 year and others offer 2 years of a comprehensive course. A third pattern is evolving that provides a foundation course focused on consumer education and personal-family relations but offers no manipulative skill experience. Building on this foundation, students may elect 1-semester depth offerings in the various areas of home economics. All programs give an increased emphasis to consumer education, management, child development, family relationships, and nutrition. Both girls and boys enroll in these programs.

In schools in some states, the comprehensive courses provide exploratory experiences in home economics occupations and careers as a contribution to career education. In all schools a central objective of the vocational home economics education program is to prepare youth for the occupation of homemaking based on the concept that husbands and wives share responsibilities in the home and that both may also work outside the home. The curriculum throughout takes into account the differing cultural and socioeconomic backgrounds of students—whether Indian, Spanish-American, Blacks, affluent or poor, rural, suburban or urban. Home economics teachers find many ways to work with the families of the students.

Upper high school offerings build on those of the early high school years. Students who have not prepared for the role of homemaker may elect combinations of depth semester courses in home economics. Many schools also offer a comprehensive course—called family living or senior homemaking—that includes the various subject-matter areas and is planned especially for mature, non-home-economics students who may soon establish their own homes.

Occupational training programs that prepare students for entry-level jobs usually begin in the eleventh grade. During the first year, students learn ways to secure and hold a job, ways to maintain good human relations on the job, principles and generalizations as well as factual information applicable to the world of work. Much of this they learn through observation and simulated experiences.

During the senior year most students spend 2 or 3 hours, 4 days a week, in a supervised work experience on jobs related to a cluster of home economics occupations. Clusters include child care services, clothing and textile services, food services, housing, home furnishings, home equipment services, and community services. Students in communities that have small numbers of trainees in any one of the clusters of home economics occupations may be placed in a variety of training stations under the supervision of a home economics coordinator and given multicluster training. Programs are adapted so that many disadvantaged and handicapped students who might otherwise be school dropouts can—with this special training—succeed in jobs.

The Future Homemakers of America (FHA) program for junior and senior high school students studying home economics provides another avenue for teaching and learning. Students have the opportunity to develop leadership ability through planning and carrying out projects in the family, school, and community. The present national program of work has two large objectives.

The first objective is to strengthen bonds between the family and community. Projects are titled: Our future as homemakers; Stable home—stable life; Make time work for you; Decisions that count.

The second objective is to help youth comprehend the problems of society and contribute to their solutions. Projects are titled: To dare is to care; Our world—a growing heritage; Preparedness—the key to opportunity.

FHA members learn about career opportunities in home economics. As a result, many future homemakers come into the profession. A new section—Home Economics Related Occupations (HERO-FHA)—has been developed for occupational home economics students.

On the postsecondary level, vocational home economics programs have expanded in consumer and homemaking education and in occupational program aspects. Many of the students in postsecondary area vocational schools and in community colleges are at the age when they marry and assume home and family responsibilities. Offerings in consumer education, family relations, child development, nutrition, and preparation for the dual role of homemaker-wage earner are particularly helpful to them. There is a growing demand for mini-courses and for courses given over a quarter or a semester. These may cover separate areas of home economics or they may be offered as comprehensive courses labeled Consumer and Family Life Skills.

Training is offered in occupational home economics, built on the programs in the secondary schools. Students may also enter the first level of training, if desired, but move beyond the entry level for placement as food service supervisor, dietary technician (if taught by a dietitian), child care/development assistant, elementary education assistant, community service worker, or specialized worker in textile and apparel industries.

Some states have begun to articulate home economics programs on the different levels. Postsecondary offerings are planned to build on high school programs and may be terminal or may give credits that students who wish to pursue further preparation in a field of study may transfer to a 4-year college program. It is hoped that the door is open at all levels to encourage students to reach a higher rung on the career ladder. Some additional training may also be available as part of adult education offerings.

Adult programs in vocational home economics contribute both to preparatory and inservice training of individuals for home economics occupations. Operators and workers in the day-care centers for children and family day care operators meet licensing requirements by enrolling in courses planned especially to meet their needs. Senior citizens, after training in child care/development may assist in day-care centers as "foster grandparents." Some states also give special training to foster parents and cottage parents. Inservice demonstration lessons and courses help to upgrade managers, cooks, and workers in school feeding programs. Nursing-home food service managers and cooks may have released time to enroll in inservice classes. Homemakers who assist social welfare workers receive training. In some states health occupations staff members and home economics educators cooperate in training homemaker-home health aides. Supervisory and executive housekeepers receive training. Many women establish their own businesses after training in textiles and clothing or in drapery and slipcover-making.

Programs focusing on consumer and homemaking skills are being "taken to the people" whenever they can be reached in groups. This technique is used especially in depressed areas where individuals are reluctant to come to the school for adult classes. One of the oldest such programs that offer homemaking classes may be found in public housing developments. The Public Housing Authority provides space, and vocational home economics provides full-time instructors to offer classes and individual consultant help. Classes are also offered for homemakers in neighborhood centers, senior citizen centers, in churches and homes, in migrants' camps, and on Indian reservations. Mobile units in some school districts are equipped as classrooms with available instructional materials. Home economics teachers drive the units; or the units are moved from place to place in order to help inner-city families, isolated rural families, migrant groups, and others who cannot come to a center. In one state, mothers are enrolled in parent education classes that parallel a cooperative nursery school program for their children. The mothers meet in churches, neighborhood centers, or elementary schools. This program reaches many families on welfare. They ask for help on consumer education, nutrition and low-cost meals (particularly those that use commodity foods and food stamps), child care, housekeeping, management, and ways to make over and alter family clothes. One of the most important outcomes of classes for homemakers from depressed areas has been the improvement of the self-concept of the women themselves. They learn that others have problems too. Some of the women are encouraged to take training and secure jobs to help improve the level of family living. The focus is on strengthening the whole family through encouragement, education, and their discovery of the resources available to them.

Depth and Relevance in Home Economics Programs

Those who plan vocational home economics programs in consumer and homemaking education consider not only the cultural and socioeconomic conditions that affect individuals and families but also the availability of jobs in the labor market and the individual needs of persons to be trained. Numerous ways have been identified to insure that programs are relevant and have depth for the persons to be served.

• **Local advisory councils,** for both consumer-homemaking education and occupational programs, consist of persons in the school and community who are in a position to identify important objectives; to support adaptations in learning experiences to meet special needs; and to offer work experience and placement opportunities for occupational students.

• **Teacher-student planning** provides an opportunity for pupil input both as to programs and objectives to be achieved in each course. The teacher's role is to define the various possibilities for learning; both youth and adult students select and add those relevant to them.

• **Parent involvement** in planning objectives, in serving as resource persons, and in helping to evaluate the effectiveness of programs in the lives of the students builds a bridge between home and school.

• **Student followup,** after the students have established their own homes or are on their own jobs, provides evaluation data and feedback as a basis for improving programs.

• **Cooperation with related agencies and organizations** concerned with the improvement of homes and families can add to the resources for teaching and give support to home economics programs offered by the school.

• **Fellow colleagues** in the school may be enlisted to assist in team-teaching areas such as consumer education or to help with occupational training programs that relate to more than one vocational area. For example, teachers of distributive education and home economics might help prepare workers for the apparel industry.

• **Use of all available resource materials** is important—particularly the materials for curriculum building and instruction that state departments of education, colleges and universities, and public and private instructional material centers are constantly developing.

Today's successful home economics teachers—whether they teach consumer and homemaking courses or occupational home economics—do not confine themselves to classroom and school only, but go out into the community to observe how families live, what people do for jobs, and what changes in society are creating pressures on individuals and families. Such teachers observe and listen to youth in order to learn to communicate with them and to offer programs that meet their needs in this time of confusing values. They relate to the people of the community and seek their assistance in planning programs that have relevance and depth.

Expansion of Vocational Home Economics

One evidence of the value of a program is the increase in numbers of persons who enroll in the program. Home economics is an elective subject in most school systems today. Over the last several years there has been an approximate 5 percent increase each year in the total number of secondary, postsecondary, and adult students who have enrolled in consumer and homemaking education programs. In fiscal year 1970, there was a total of 2,419,216 enrolled. Of these, 227,972 were youths and adults living in depressed areas. This figure was an increase from 46,393 in fiscal year 1969. Enrollment figures are not available for those schools that offer consumer and homemaking education programs without the help of federal funds. The membership of the Future Homemakers of America has grown to over 500,000 junior and senior high school students, the largest youth organization in the secondary schools.

In the occupational home economics programs there have been large gains in enrollments since the passage of the 1963 Vocational Education Act. In fiscal year 1965, there were 1,500 enrolled and in fiscal year 1970 there were 151,194. According to predictions, this number will continue to increase rapidly for several years.

The number of boys and men enrolled in vocational home economics has also been increasing. In fiscal year 1970, of the total enrollment, 13 percent were males.

Consumer and homemaking education is the only subject area offered by the schools that focuses entirely on the purpose of assisting consumers and improving home environments and the quality of family life. All students could profit from enrolling in some aspect of homemaking. Occupational home economics is the only vocational education area that focuses totally on training of personnel who provide services to individuals and to homes and families. With the nation's increased interest in strengthening family life, in enriching the early years of childhood, and in meeting the needs of older citizens, the demands for home economics programs and enrollments should continue to increase.

Challenges Ahead

If the profession is to maintain the thrust of vocational home economics and to expand and adapt to continued changes in needs of individuals and families, these challenges must be met:

• The challenge to continue to find new ways of offering programs so as to reach a greater number of youths and adults than are reached at present. Mini-courses, individualized instruction, use of educational technology, and new avenues for taking the program to the people will help make this goal possible.

• The challenge to teach so that there are observable differences in those being taught—for example, evidences that they have become more competent homemakers and family members or more successful on the jobs for which they were trained. Accountability of instruction is essential.

• The challenge to make changes in teacher education on the preservice and inservice levels so that teacher quality continues to improve and varied types of home economics teachers are available.

• The challenge to increase the resources allocated to research to provide firm data as bases for decisions related to program planning, instruction, and the evaluation of program effectiveness.

• The challenge to analyze needs, determine priorities, and maximize resources within the limits of reduced resources in many state departments of education and in colleges and universities. These actions are necessary to provide leadership and supervision to help teachers strive continuously to improve the quality of their instruction.

Both the challenges and the opportunities are many for vocational home economics to contribute to the continuous improvement of the home and the family.

References

1. Public Law 88-210, December 18, 1963. *Vocational Education Act of 1963*, Amendments to George Barden and Smith Hughes Vocational Education Acts, p. 9.

2. Public Law 90-576, October 16, 1968. *Vocational Education Amendments of 1968*, Title I, Part B, p. 9.

3. *Ibid.*, Title I, Part F, p. 22.

4. Bureau of Adult, Vocational, and Library Programs, U.S. Department of Health, Education, and Welfare. *Regulations for State Plan Programs*, Vocational Education Amendments of 1968. Washington, D.C., April 1969, p. 10. (Material for administrative use only.)

5. Part in parentheses added in Public Law 91-230; H.R. 514, April 13, 1970, p. 69.

6. Marland, S. P., Jr., "Career Education," from a speech given before the Thirty-third Session of the International Conference on Education, Geneva, Switzerland, September 15-23, 1971.

19

Home Economics—
New Directions II

Gordon Bivens, Margaret Fitch, Gwendolyn Newkirk, Beatrice Paolucci, Em Riggs, Satenig St. Marie, Gladys Vaughn

Introduction

The committee to develop a new statement for our profession has completed its work, and the final statement—which is printed here in full—will be available in quantity in June. Copies will be on display in the AHEA booth at annual meeting in San Antonio.

This statement has had much input from Association members. The first and second drafts were printed in newsletters inserted in the *Journal of Home Economics* in January and May, 1974. A hearing was held at the 1974 Annual Meeting in Los Angeles, when state associations and individual members had an opportunity to present their viewpoints to the committee. In early February, members of the committee met to rewrite the statement, based on all of the suggestions received. HOME ECONOMICS - NEW DIRECTIONS II is a result of that meeting. It is really a labor of love.

Just as the original "New Directions," written in 1959, recognized the strengths of this profession and outlined new directions for home economics on its 50th anniversary, so, too, hopefully, this NEW DIRECTIONS II will provide leadership to the profession at a time when the interplays between family and society call for new insights and new emphases.

In addition, the statement of purpose and historical perspective should give insight about home economics to those outside the profession.

NEW DIRECTIONS II is not intended to be a final statement about home economics, but rather a new benchmark at this point in the development of the profession. The statement should be reviewed continually and hopefully other committees to come will rewrite it to keep us in tune with the times.

Whether or not this statement serves the profession well will depend on the willingness of each individual home economist to evaluate his or her current work against the benchmark goals, to do some personal and professional value clarification about the suggested new priorities, to be willing to eliminate some things, to change others, and to innovate programs that respond to these goals. Only when this kind of substantive change takes place within the profession can this NEW DIRECTIONS II be considered an important contribution to the profession.

Historical Perspective

The founders of the profession defined the field thus:

> "Home Economics in its most comprehensive sense is the study of the laws, conditions, principles, and ideals which are concerned on the one hand with man's immediate physical environment and on the other hand, with his nature as a social being, and is the study *especially* of the relation between these two factors. . . ."

Although the nature of the field has evolved, its basic mission remains essentially the same today.

Statement of Purpose

The focus of home economics is family in its various forms. Family is defined as a unit of intimate, transacting, and interdependent persons who share some values and goals, resources, responsibility for decisions, and have commitment to one another over time.

HOME ECONOMICS views the family as a major source of nurturance, protection, and renewal for the individual. As an educational force, the family significantly contributes to the qualitive development of its individual members and has the potential to prepare them for effective productivity for self and society.

From this perspective, HOME ECONOMICS works through family to effect an optimum balance between people and their environments. HOME ECONOMICS accepts the challenge of helping people to adjust to change and to shape the future.

The core of HOME ECONOMICS is the family ecosystem. It is the study of the reciprocal relations of family to its natural and man-made environments, the effect of these singly or in unison as they shape the internal functioning of families, and the interplays between the family and other social institutions and the physical environment.

New Priorities for Home Economics

These statements assume that the home economics profession recognizes the interrelationship of theory (a knowledge base for home economics) and research (scientifically structured investigations about the family ecosystem). Theory and research provide the base for application in business, education, and service programs. The implications (costs/benefits assessed in terms of people and environments) for maintaining and/or changing the family unit need to be continuously assessed in charting the future.

It is not intended that the following priorities be all-inclusive. Rather, the home economist will adapt and expand the statements to give more substantive meaning for particular situations, interests, and needs.

1. *Futuristic Thinking and Planning.* Invisions alternative designs of every-day living and critically evaluates and interprets the costs/benefits of these. For example:
   - reshaping values
   - assuring optimum human development and viable environments
   - recognizing the relationship of private and public decisions.

2. *Public Policy Formation.* Achieves greater input into decisions made in the public realm that impact on families. For example:
   - providing empirical data that identifies consequences of procedures, programs, and policies
   - serving as an advocate for the family
   - using commensurate political techniques to bring about change.

3. *Creative Adaptation to Uncertainty and Change.* Views the opportunities inherent in change and is willing to assume risks in directing change affecting families. For example:
   - taking a stand on controversial issues in one's professional role
   - accepting conflict as an effective mode for clarifying values
   - pioneering new professional dimensions in response to change

4. *Redistribution of Resources.* Recognizes the interdependence of resource availability and the development of human potentials, and initiates actions that lead to a more equitable resource distribution. For example:
   - developing programs on population education
   - examining effects of resource limitations on human behavior

5. *Interrelatedness of the Professional and the Paraprofessional.* Distinguishes between the competencies of the professional and the paraprofessional and acknowledges the contributions of each to families. For example:

- identifying the competences required and education needed for each role
- matching the role to the needs.

These priorities are only viable when home economists critically examine the profession in relation to existing programs to ensure that they are justifiable; as changes are effected, do the existing programs require different structures and emphases or mere additions to present situations? The home economist must be creative and innovative in accepting the challenges that new priorities require new structures, programs, and responsibilities.

This statement has evolved from many issues raised by AHEA members at this point in time (1974-75). It represents the reflection of their concerns and their recognition of the continuing need for redirection of priorities of the profession to meet the changing needs of family and society.

20

A Statement by the Vocational Education Coalition

Alberta D. Hill, Twyla Shear, Camille G. Bell, Aleene A. Cross, Enid A. Carter, and Leora N. Horning

A coalition of the three professional organizations concerned with vocational home economics education—the American Home Economics Association (AHEA), the American Vocational Association (AVA), and the Home Economics Education Association (HEEA)—was established by governing bodies of those organizations in May 1977. Each association selected two representatives. The general purpose of the Vocational Education Coalition is to increase communication and to project a unified thrust and focus on issues related to vocational home economics education.

The six members of the Coalition have reviewed their charge and agreed upon the following purposes.

• Maintain continuous dialogue among professional organizations concerned with vocational home economics education.

• Identify existing and potential issues of vocational home economics education.

• Develop a statement regarding vocational home economics education that will serve as a baseline for the analysis of future positions.

• Review positions on current issues relating to vocational home economics education and facilitate development of consensus among the organizations.

• Determine various target groups to which issues and positions concerning vocational home economics education should be communicated.

The Coalition has accepted the following assumptions as guidelines for its operation.

• Coalition members are responsible for consulting with the officers and staff of the organization they represent and for reflecting the philosophy and purpose of that organization to the Coalition.

• The governing board and staff of each organization is responsible for communicating and clarifying to each new group of officers and relevant committees the position and purposes of the Coalition.

• The Coalition is to serve as a clearinghouse for policy or position statements developed by any one of the organizations.

• Consensus on a position reached by the Coalition will be communicated to the governing boards of the three organizations.

• When consensus cannot be reached, each organization may explore its own alternative positions with policymakers, designating these positions as its own point of view and presenting both the rationales and reasons for differences among the organizations. Such alternative positions are to be shared with other professional organizations through the Coalition.

Scope and Definition of Vocational Home Economics Education

Vocational home economics education prepares males and females for the occupation of homemaking and paid employment in home economics occupations. For the purpose of this paper, the term *vocational homemaking education* is used as a generic term for programs now designated in legislation as "consumer and homemaking" programs. *Vocational home economics education* is used as a more general term to include both wage earning and homemaking programs and to describe professional educators.

Occupation of Homemaking

The occupation of homemaking requires knowledge and skills that are interrelated and necessary for optimum quality of life for individuals and families. Values, management, and interpersonal relationships are major concepts that unify the content of the subject-matter areas of child and family development, clothing and textiles, foods and nutrition, consumer education and resource management, and housing.

The essential skills of homemaking include (1) providing for personal and family development at various stages of the life cycle and establishing satisfying personal and family relationships; (2) nurturing children; (3) providing nutritious food for family members; (4) selecting and maintaining housing and living environments for family members; (5) providing and caring for family clothing; and (6) managing financial and other resources. There are additional skills that may be considered home economics content but if such skills are not essential for the occupation of homemaking, they should not be included in vocational homemaking education.

Relationship of Paid Employment and Homemaking

Home economics occupations for paid employment apply knowledge and skills related to the above subject-matter areas. The concepts and applications basic to preparing for the occupation of homemaking are basic to the home economics occupations classified as paid employment. For example, the same clothing principles can be used by the homemaker that are used in the apparel industry. The human development and care principles that apply to paid care for children, the elderly, and the handicapped apply to caring for one's own family as well. The difference lies in the setting, the instructional objectives, the level of competency and responsibility required, and the scope of operation. This overlap remains a strength and a link between preparation programs for paid employment and for the occupation of homemaking.

Funding and Structure for Vocational Home Economics

Recognition of the relationship of well-ordered, quality home and family life to productive, satisfying work life is implicit, if not explicit, in the history of vocational education legislation. From the earliest legislation supporting vocational education to the present, Congress has included funding for home economics education. The funding for the occupation of homemaking implies acknowledgement of the fundamental importance of family life and the functioning of households to the economic, social, and political well-being of our nation.

From the Smith-Hughes Act of 1917 to the Vocational Act of 1963 and subsequent amendments of 1968, 1972, and 1976, legislation has evolved from a focus on developing manpower to meet the needs of industrial and corporate society to emphasizing the human needs of persons, including the need for occupational competence. Many factors during that 60-year period affected the legislative priorities: a major depression; wars; dramatic technological changes; changes both in numbers and age proportions of the population; increased standard of living and economic security; increased numbers of persons in school and increased level of education for the population as a whole; social and governmental action to ensure full and equal rights of opportunity under the law to all persons regardless of age, sex, race, or religion; and a phenomenal increase in the proportion of women entering the work force.

A pervasive trend throughout this period has been the government role as intervenor to enhance the human condition. Sixty years of vocational education legislation reflects this.

Current Needs

Federal support for vocational home economics education is needed more than ever to meet the stated and implicit goals of government and education. Although the dollar amounts funded have increased since 1963, they have not kept pace with inflation. In addition, funding never has reached authorization levels, in spite of heightened sensitivity to serious problems related to family and household functions.

Homemaking functions are increasingly cognitive and complex and not likely to be learned in the contemporary home and family setting without some intervention. Kenneth Boulding (1), an economist, said that one of the greatest weaknesses in our social structure is the household decision maker's lack of skill. In traditional homes the skills were passed down from one generation to the next, but not so today. Boulding recommends a high priority for household education.

> If we had any adequate sense of the priorities of our society, it seems to me that we would put ten times as much of both research and education into the area of household as we do now (I)."

With about half of all adult women in the work force, there is an unprecedented need for education of both men and women to help these working women with childrearing and other family responsibilities. Now is the time for full support for vocational home economics education.

In the federal government there is much interest in funding to ameliorate acute family-related social problems. However, efforts tend to be fragmented and overlook established programs and delivery systems such as the secondary and postsecondary schools. The established systems can address emerging problems effectively and at less cost in time and dollars than development of a new bureaucracy.

Home economics educators urge three governmental actions: (1) full funding to the extent authorized by law for education in the occupation of homemaking; (2) continuation of categorical funding or other legislative assurance of education for the occupation of homemaking; and (3) strengthening of the established delivery system.

Why Homemaking Education?

The family, or household, is a major institution of society for socializing the young. In addition to its educative and protective function, the family system interacts with the other major institutions of society. If the family system does not function, then other systems such as formal education and the business society will break down (1,2).

Problems such as malnutrition, child abuse, consumer fraud, teenage pregnancy, energy waste, and environmental pollution, which are among our nation's most intense social concerns, all bear on the family. The habits and values of persons related to these matters generally are "caught" in the home and family context. But economic, technological, political, and social forces have resulted in changes that have increased the complexity of choice and the burden on families to make informed choices. Therefore, the family system must be supported in its role for sustaining our society.

To be fully human no one can be exempted from interdependence with other persons. Each person needs basic competencies in interpersonal skills and resource management related to home and family to live a satisfying life regardless of the living style chosen. The sharing of home tasks in the household is an inevitable outcome of women working outside the home in paid employment. Both men and women have been conditioned culturally to perceive homemaking as women's work. However, the competencies and attitudes necessary for homemaker roles are learned, and these can and should be learned by both men and women. The increasing complexity and changing character of homemaking roles and tasks seem to require organized opportunities for learning these tasks.

Funding for the Occupation of Homemaking

The major funds for most school programs are now the responsibility of state governments. State and local funds are needed for the regular maintenance and expansion of programs. Recognizing the added cost of vocational education, states have provided supplementary funding for vocational programs including vocational home economics.

In the past, federal funds have been used to equalize the opportunities for vocational education among the states. This should be a continued goal for federal funding. However, the most important reason for federal funding is that certain national goals can be achieved best if there is federal support. National goals such as equity of entry and education for teenage parents may not be accepted by certain states or communities because of cultural and economic histories. These states or communities need to be encouraged; federal dollars are needed to stimulate state funding. National goals related to vocational home economics programs include such social concerns as nutritional status, well-being of children, equal opportunities for minorities and the handicapped, and consumer rights and responsibilities.

Home economics is unique in its need for added support at the federal level. Although the Education Amendments of 1976 define work as paid and

167

unpaid employment, the predominant focus of vocational education has been to prepare persons to earn a living. Although the occupation of homemaking is generally accepted as being essential for maintaining the family as the basic unit of society, it is more difficult to quantify the economic worth of this occupation than other occupations for which vocational training is provided. Some progress is being made in public recognition of the economic contribution of homemaking, but the educational and social contributions of the home still are not given the same value among many people as those activities that lead to a specific wage, salary, or profit.

It can be said, therefore, that homemakers have been discriminated against. It is as much the federal government's responsibility to provide support for homemaking education as it is to provide funds for other programs designed to eliminate descrimination. One way for the nation to affirm its belief that family functions and education for family life are worthy is to continue funding consumer and homemaking education and to add incentive monies for particularly critical areas of concern.

For federal funds to be used to achieve national goals, some program guidance must be developed at the national level. Such guidance should be flexible enough to allow for adaptation to specific state and local needs, but there must be some assurance that the monies will be used to achieve national goals.

Vocational homemaking education requires a federal-state-local partnership. The citizens of the community served by a school need to be involved in decisions related to the scope and content of the curriculum, the organization and structure of the program, the facilities to be used, and the qualifications of the teachers. However, it is difficult for local groups to assume full responsibility for these decisions because they lack the professional expertise needed to evaluate and revise programs continually, based on new knowledge and social, economic, and political changes. State governments are being asked to assume more of the responsibility for funding local school programs, and states rather than local educational agencies have the responsibility for setting standards for education and licensing or certifying school personnel.

The Delivery System for Homemaking Education

All persons should have the opportunity to participate in educational programs that prepare them for the roles of homemaking. This proposition suggests that such education should be provided in a number of institutions, agencies, and organizations within our society. It should be kept in mind, however, that to provide a continuous and regular educational program, the well-established and tested delivery systems should be used. Vocational home economics education in the public schools, including postsecondary and adult programs, is one such well-established system.

School systems are the institutions in our society that still reach most people and have a continuing organized system for the delivery of an educational program. Public schools have provided and can continue to provide both specific courses and comprehensive programs for regularly enrolled students and informal education programs for youth and adults. The schools also sponsor the student organization Future Homemakers of America (FHA/HERO), which has become a valuable vehicle for preparing youth for roles in homemaking and home economics-related occupations. It seems logical to conclude, therefore, that if a home economics education program is to reach all people, it must be continued through the public school system.

Society generally has viewed homemaking as females' work and home economics as a field of study for females. Thus, male students may not be enrolled in homemaking courses and may miss the opportunity to prepare for parenting, consumer decision making, and nutrition. However, when sexism is eliminated, it is possible for homemaking education courses to serve everybody. Homemaking education cannot reach all students when (1) facilities or number of teachers are limited; (2) the program is not truly a vocational program, but includes specific skills interesting to only a part of the school population; and (3) any group is discouraged from enrolling.

Federal Role

Federal vocational education funding, beginning in 1917, has assisted in developing a federal-state-local communication system that has given continuity and stability to home economics programs provided by schools. This structure has had some weaknesses and needs to be reviewed and updated constantly to ensure that it is working effectively and efficiently. Discarding or dismantling the system, however, is not the way to improve it. This federal, state, and local cooperative effort has enabled states to work together on research, needs assessment, and curriculum development; enabled teachers, teacher educators, and supervisors to combine efforts for program development and improvement; and has established a network of communication that is used by other educational agencies and organizations for communicating with home economists.

Preparation of Teachers and Leaders

To maintain strong programs in vocational home economics education, the teacher educators who prepare the teachers, local and state supervisors of vocational home economics programs, and the curriculum developers for these programs must have a background of experience and training in home economics. Although team teaching of some aspects of vocational homemaking programs may use the expertise of teachers in other fields, all programs that are directed toward developing skills for the occupation of homemaking must be the responsibility of teachers with an orientation to all aspects of managing home responsibilities.

The preparation of home economics educators is vital to vocational home economics education. Certain competencies, including those in general education, specialized education, and professional education, are essential for teachers and leaders in vocational home economics education. General education competencies are based on the supporting disciplines of physical, biological, social, and behavioral sciences, the arts, and humanities. The specialization competencies are derived from all subject-matter areas of home economics. The professional competencies encompass knowledge and skills of the teaching and learning process.

Those individuals preparing to teach vocational home economics education should have learned the concept that all subject-matter areas of home economics are interrelated and must be meshed together. This concept is essential for those who teach the occupation of homemaking since effective programs in vocational homemaking education must consider the complete realm of maintaining homes, which involves the interaction of consumer education, nutrition, food usage, clothing, care and guidance of children, management of household tasks and finances, housing, values, and interpersonal relations.

Home economists who teach wage-earning courses need specialized preparation and appropriate occupational experience. There must be assurances that these programs are carried out intelligently by qualified vocational home economics educators.

Competencies Needed

Competencies in each subject-matter area of home economics must be demonstrated by individuals preparing to teach vocational home economics education. Prevailing social, economic, and technological conditions in our society that affect the occupation of homemaking demand special emphases on certain aspects of subject matter. Needs and interests of special groups should be considered in determining the present and projected competencies needed by vocational home economics teachers.

It is extremely important to know how to teach as well as what to teach. There are some basic professional competencies for vocational homemaking teachers that are similar to those for all teachers. These include fulfilling professional roles, establishing interpersonal relationships, planning a total specialized program, managing a total program, providing instruction, guiding students in personal and professional development, and using appropriate evaluative procedures.

In addition to these basic professional competencies, there are competencies unique to vocational home economics teachers. These include the ability to:

- assess the needs of the people to be served through working with advisory committees, conducting surveys, and making home and family contacts;
  - comprehend the principles and philosophy of vocational education;
  - relate legislative program purposes to specific community needs;
  - integrate the subject-matter areas of home economics as they relate to the occupation of homemaking;
  - demonstrate essential skills required by the occupation of homemaking or for specific occupations related to home economics;
  - direct out-of-class experiences for individual students that relate to appropriate aspects of the occupation; and
  - integrate the activities of FHA/HERO with the total vocational home economics program to achieve the overall objective.

Responsibility for Professional Development

The U.S. Office of Education, state education agencies, colleges and universities, and professional organizations all have a role in the professional preparation and continuing development of home economics educators. The education program specialist for vocational home economics education in the Office of Education can help provide leadership in professional development through national and regional meetings that focus on trends and issues inherent in teacher education. The Office of Education can also help provide consistency by establishing national goals for the programs.

State education agencies have been given the responsibility for establishing and maintaining standards and certifying teachers. These agencies ensure that certification for vocational home economics teachers responds to state needs and state and national legislative purposes. Leadership for in-service education of teachers also is assumed by the state education agency in cooperation with colleges and universities. Local and state supervisors of vocational home economics also must have input into planning and assessing teacher education programs. It is, therefore, imperative for these administrators to have an educational background and experience in home economics.

Four-year institutions of higher education should continue to provide preservice education for vocational home economics teachers. It is the responsibility of colleges and universities preparing these teachers to employ teacher educators who have a background of experience and training in home economics since this is the field of study that provides the expertise needed for vocational home economics programs. Comprehensive education in each subject-matter area should be provided in preservice education, and the concept of the interrelatedness of all home economics subject matter should be emphasized. While specialization is necessary for the teacher of home economics-related occupations, the curriculum of vocational homemaking teachers must remain comprehensive and interrelated.

Professional organizations serve to keep members up-to-date in basic professional competencies. Professional organizations provide opportunities for members to assume leadership in implementing the legislative purposes of vocational home economics and in interpreting the program to the public.

The Coalition is responsible for coordinating vocational home economics education efforts for AHEA, AVA, and HEEA. These organizations must be in accord with each other to project a united position to policymakers at local, state, and national levels. Such unity will have a far-reaching effect on outstanding, innovative vocational home economics education programs throughout the nation.

References

1. Boulding, K.E. "The Household as Achilles Heel." *Journal of Consumer Affairs* 6: 110-119; Winter 1972.

2. Boulding, K.E. "An Economist's View." In *Ethics and Business*. University Park, PA.: Center for Research, College of Business. Pennsylvania State University, 1962.

Home Economics: Proud Past—Promising Future 1984 AHEA Commemorative Lecture

Marjorie M. Brown

Unlike a mere chronicle of events, history of home economics makes intelligible past actions of home economists so that we understand where we are today and how we got there. But our purpose is not to live in the past—to revel in past achievements; it is to comprehend and profit from our mistakes for, if we are intelligent, we do not have to continue those mistakes. History as past happenings is sometimes referred to as "a series of messes" (1). But it is only through historical analysis that we see how we got into the present mess—and how we may be able to get out of it. Such venerable age as the 75th birthday of AHEA and at least the 110th anniversary of home economics in colleges and universities suggests that we be reflective about our past and our present in order to consider our future with enlightenment.

What I shall try to do is to develop a fuller consciousness of what has happened in home economics, the how and why of where we are today, and what we need to do about it. But because of the limitation of time, I am afraid the consciousness will be small—and a little consciousness is a dangerous thing. My interpretations today may seem arbitrary because there is not the time to document them and to ground them in reasons. But today's interpretations are drawn from a detailed historical study of home economics in the United States, which is fully documented and grounded (and which is to be published later this year) (2).

History of Home Economics

I do not believe that, as home economists generally, we understand the history of our own profession. Rather, we have tended to make that history into a myth. Part of my purpose is to de-mythologize our history.

There are a number of things in our history in which we can take pride. For example, over time there have been enlightened, rational, and competent leaders and critics in home economics of whom we may rightly be proud:

Marion Talbot, Alice Chown (a Canadian home economist), Benjamin Andrews, Lita Bane, Effie I. Raitt, Flora Rose, Hazel Kyrk, Grace Henderson, Ruth Lehman, Dorothy Scott, and Margaret Justin. There were others, too, who appeared in the limelight only briefly but whose insightful exposure of professional realities could have brought the profession into closer harmony with the real interests of individuals and the family. But home economists have been blind and deaf to these insightful in-house critics. Unreflectively we have as a group, with individual exceptions, followed a Pied Piper who has expected and received from us dogmatic, uncomprehending compliance.

Especially in our early years there were accomplishments: success in having the potential of home economics recognized in American society during the late nineteenth and early twentieth centuries; success in developing a network of programs and institutional affiliations throughout the nation; expanse in numbers of programs and numbers of home economists. But these were quantitative achievements based on the potential we promised: to fulfill the potential promises, qualitative accomplishments were needed.

Early Potential of Home Economics

There was recognition in the late nineteenth century of the negative effects of existing social realities on the individual and the family. The plight of the individual in an increasingly industrial and urban society, dominated by powerful economic forces that contributed to disintegration of both family and community, was recognized. It was seen by many of those early home economists that education was needed to create a home life that would both enhance the development of the individual and contribute to a more democratic society. To provide such education was the original mission of home economics. This was the aim that underlay many of the early programs established in colleges and universities; others, however, were dedicated to the crafts and technical skills of the household. Those who came initially to the early Lake Placid Conference were also concerned by "the sociologic problem of the family" prompted by recognition of the effects of an industrial society on the family and its ability to protect and nurture the individual. It was in the first few meetings at Lake Placid that the earlier statement of aim of home economics was reiterated. Further, in those early meetings, the subject matter of home economics was to be interdisciplinary, drawing upon philosophy (including ethics), history, literature, and the social and natural sciences.

What happened at Lake Placid, however, was ironic because the views that came to dominate later meetings of the conference led toward a subject matter and professional practice directly contrary to the earlier commitments of mission and of interdisciplinarity. It is important for us to understand what occurred at Lake Placid and how it occurred because the dominant views and contradictions that made home economists then victims of their own logic are still with us today. We have not changed fundamentally in our ways of thinking and our mode of action in this century.

The Lake Placid Conference: Its Influence on Thought and Action in Home Economics

First, I would like to make clear that there was not harmony among Lake Placid Conference participants regarding the view of human beings, of the family, and of society, the meaning of rationality, the ends to be served through educative activity in home economics, the view of knowledge for home economics, or the organization of the discipline.

On the one side were Ellen H. Richards, Melvil Dewey, and Alice P. Norton, among others, who were less vocal, whose viewpoint dominated the conference. On the other side were Alice Chown, Marion Talbot, and Benjamin Andrews as well as a number of other participants and invited speakers. I will try to contrast these views briefly in table 1.

It is helpful to place the dominant view at the Lake Placid Conference, that is, that of Mrs. Richards, in its larger historical-social context. It was the Victorian period in American history. Victorian Americans were highly class conscious: They had a vertical view of society in which there was both eagerness to climb upward and constant fear of falling. One way of climbing was to become a professional; even homemaking was to be professionalized. Another way of climbing was through "the management of things" in making the home a place of business and industrial efficiency—the naive notion that moral, intellectual, and aesthetic conditions, including those in the home, would be better if physical and economic conditions were improved.

Consistent with upward climbing was the inclination to jump on the bandwagon of modernization. Many Victorian Americans held the notion that social revolution is a natural process of improvement and progress. Mrs. Richards was a strong proponent of this view and believed that "modern" ideas and all social change constitute progress; therefore, it behooves the individual and the family to conform to modernization and to the existing society. Outstanding in modern developments of the time were three: an increasingly bureaucratic structure in society, the rapid growth of technology under the auspices of corporate industry, and an adulation for empirical science that contributed to the other two developments.

Society was becoming increasingly bureaucratic, and bureaucratic ideas prevailed: administrative control through management, administrative efficiency, fragmented division of work, social engineering. These ideas were consistent with the existing social structure in which corporate industry and business were gaining control of social and political processes. Historians of the period document the capture of higher education by the engineers whose

175

interests were with industry and concerned with fitting people into an industrial society (3). While Mrs. Richards verbally berated the orientation of business and industry toward competition, greed, power, and exploitation, she embraced the "management" values in their procedures, which upheld the very norms she berated. Together with Melvil Dewey, she stood for technical education "in the management of things" and was a strong proponent of "social engineering" in which families and the public were to be manipulated by technical-scientific experts.

The Victorian period in America was also one in which there was adulation for empirical science that, in Melvil Dewey's words, would "cure all evils" through a technocratic politics. This adulation was one in which the positivistic view of science promoted by Comte was adopted. It was not that empirical science was to replace superstition and mere opinion in factual claims; it was that empirical science was to be the only rational way of knowing. Thus language and concepts, norms for regulating social life, and the processes and standards for communicating in everyday life were placed outside the bounds of rationality. This "scientistic" view ignored the fact that these latter structures of rationality had been established in traditions of the culture long before the method of empirical science was adopted. Mrs. Richards described herself as "one with faith in science as a cure-all" (4). She stood for home economics as "utilization of all the resources of modern science to improve the home life" in which home life would be "unhampered by traditions of the past" (5). What she did not recognize was that we would grow up in a world without meaning and without norms for thought and action if there were no traditions.

The historian Wiebe has characterized theoretical activity of the late nineteenth and early twentieth centuries in America as unreflective. Speaking of theorists of the time, he said:

> Perhaps they accepted ideas indiscriminately . . . By failing to probe the implications of their own ideas, they opened themselves to any number of thoughtless shifts in emphasis. Too often they followed the glittering phrase and the bright hope without testing its substance (6).

This snatching of untested ideas and "glittering phrases" from a variety of sources was upheld by Mrs. Richards and Mr. Dewey. When challenged by Alice Chown on this point, the *Proceedings* of the conference show: "Mr. Dewey and the chairman (Mrs. Richards) expressed themselves in favor of gleaning ideas wherever found, of keeping abreast of the times" (7).

But "keeping up" with new ideas did not include comprehending and evaluating their implications. Thus it was easy for Mrs. Richards and her followers to accept ideological beliefs promoted by dominant social groups to maintain the existing power structure.

We cannot leave the dominant view at the Lake Placid Conference without reflecting upon the rationality that prevailed. Rationality in communication often did not exist. Mrs. Richards did not engage in rational argumentation with other members of the conference when her claims to truth, to rightness of norms, or to the clarity of her conceptions were questioned. She did not provide a clear set of reasons to support a position she took although there are scattered hints that enable us to see what her presuppositions were. She had a way of ignoring views and beliefs contrary to her own and of technically "managing" the conference so that such views would be given minimal if any consideration, as examination of the transcript of certain sessions indicates.

Power was important to Mrs. Richards by her own words as well as by Caroline Hunt's description of her (8). Her leadership was authoritarian, and there was a certain arrogance in assuming her own infallibility when a number of other conference participants clearly were more enlightened about social realities and had more adequate conceptual schemata for developing a profession and a discipline than she. But it was authoritarianism with a friendly face because a number of conference participants admired her leadership—perhaps because they were dependent on a leader of their own thinking, perhaps because she echoed popular views, and perhaps because she had a certain charisma among Victorian women. But charismatic leadership, which encourages dependence, must be distinguished from competent rational leadership, which seeks to develop the intellectual and social capacities of a group (including the "leaders").

Earlier I commented that the ways of thinking and the mode of action that dominated the Lake Placid Conference have continued in home economics. Time does not permit considering the periods from the Lake Placid Conference to the present time although I have done so in the longer study. Here I will have to limit to showing how the ways of thinking and acting dominant at the beginning of the century are still with us.

Legacy of Lake Placid Conference Reflected in Present-Day Thought, Action

I believe that home economists wish to see themselves as responsible professionals, capable of reason, and freely choosing as a profession what is done in its discipline and in its practice. But the ways of thinking and acting, which dominated the Lake Placid Conference, have become so taken for granted that we do not recognize our own self-contradictions nor our failure to be loyal to our own aspirations. First, let us see how we have become frozen into the patterns of thought and action that prevailed at the beginning of the twentieth century.

Continuation of Patterns
of Thought and Action

Certain major points of the dominant position at Lake Placid are still with us.

1. *Low opinion of human nature.* We hold that human beings, including home economists, are not capable of complex conceptual activity—of forming complex concepts and beliefs that enter into complex desires and intentions; that they are capable of revising previous concepts, beliefs, desires, and intentions on the basis of reflective experience; or that they are capable of self-understanding and of changing themselves based upon that understanding. *Evidence:* We expect people, including ourselves as home economists, to be passive recipients of information. We have done this by limiting the form of rationality in home economics to that which produces information from observation and technical how-to-do-it rules. We accept as given the social realities that are observable without considering their human implications and the possibility of a more humane society.

Take, for example, the recent endorsement of the "information society" by some home economists. By implication, this endorsement assumes that forms of cognitive activity other than passive reception of information, selected and directed by others, are either impossible or undesirable. Thus we deny those we presume to serve the development of those capacities that make them autonomous persons: the formation and validation of complex concepts, the rational social processes of agreement on norms of conduct, learning and using the complexities of language and speech competently, rational argumentation regarding the validity of claims to truth, to rightness, to adequacy of concepts, to sincerity in what is said or done. We even deny these to ourselves, both in the kind of "education" we expect of home economics professionals and the kind of professional meetings we have where we go home with the same old concepts and the same old patterns of thinking with which we came.

It is no secret that a great many home economists are threatened by and avoid complex thought that involves their willingness to reason; we have encouraged among us a dogmatism and dependence on "leaders." There is no better evidence of this than the way in which revisions of the mission of home economics are accepted. We do not comprehend what it is that is revised nor do we comprehend and validate a new statement of mission. Thus we dogmatically accept what is short enough to memorize without understanding or caring about its implications.

2. *Conformity to existing society.* We continue, like Mrs. Richards, to emphasize conformity to the existing society. We do this without really comprehending and evaluating the social realities to which we expect conformity. We continue to adopt "new ideas" indiscriminately, and we seek to emulate the dominant forces in society, that is, the class in power. *Evidence:* Approval

of the "information society" already mentioned, our involvement with futurism, our overly late acknowledgement of the feminist movement (waiting until it was socially acceptable), our upholding and promoting externally formed standards for home life from the mass culture controlled by industry, our involvement in politics as participation in centralized policymaking that depoliticizes citizens—because that is the way politics operate today, our view of leadership in the profession as business management (which dominates social processes today)—for example, the workshops on leadership training.

We have never initiated or championed an unpopular political-moral cause or been willing to enter into political conflict in behalf of that cause; we want what is socially safe and will not rock the boat. Ours is a class society, and we are still very class conscious. We correctly identify corporate business as the dominant class and we seek to emulate this class. *Examples:* Recent articles in *AHEA Action* on climbing the corporate ladder (home economists in "top jobs"), using the methods of corporate business to "promote" home economics (public relations and advertising), high-status people in the culture industry invited to be major speakers at meetings, even the class system we establish in our own professional organization with a board of directors and VIP lounges and VIP luncheons at meetings.

3. *Viewing the home in physicalistic terms.* Many of us still view the home, as did Ellen G. Richards, in physicalistic and economic terms of the management of "things." We still hold on to a nineteenth-century view known as *economic materialism*, which holds that physical and economic conditions in the society and in the home naturally precede improvement of the political-moral, the social-psychological, and the cultural. *Evidence:* We endorse a political economy in our country, including the current welfare system, without recognizing the human effects or doing anything politically to remove the social causes of poverty; much of the subject matter of home economics places emphasis on the control of things without giving attention to social forces that control the distribution of things; those in specializations on "things" in the home have little or no educational background that enables them to understand human thought or communication and action in the family where "things" are not separated from their meaning in sociocultural life and from the political-moral struggle.

But many or most American families are ahead of us on this: They realize that their possession of things is not a sufficient condition to make or break the success of the family as a social institution nor the happiness of its members. Perhaps that is why to many in our society, home economics has become an anachronism. (Please note that I have not said that there is no place for things in the home. I have said that we have an oversimplified conceptual scheme regarding their place and have overemphasized their technical control when we view them only in physicalistic terms.)

4. *Adulation of empirical science and technology.* As home economists, we continue to worship empirical science and technology. To some of us, we would be purer in character if we were limited to natural science and technology. But analytic-empirical science also dominates the social and psychological study of the family, and we dispense technical information about how the family can control its social life. Evidence of this adulation is in how often we see the word *science* added to specializations in home economics: food sciences, consumer sciences, family social science, management science, et cetera. It is also evidenced in what we consider research to be as reflected over the years in the contents of our two journals. Our preoccupation with technology is equally evident: our devotion to new products resulting from technology (for example, in exhibits for and about home economics), our love of techniques in providing information about household tasks and family life, in teaching, communication, counseling, "promoting" home economics. But it is not merely the adulation of empirical science and technology of which we should be aware; we need to be critically conscious of the consequences to us and to those we seek to serve professionally.

The one-dimensional view of knowledge as empirical science and of rational action as using efficient means to produce given results, known as positivism, has had its consequences. Because it is one-dimensional, it has closed out the older intellectual traditions of standards and procedures for rational social argumentation as inquiry into conceptual meanings and into the norms that regulate interpersonal relations and social conduct. The language of science is artificial, and its concepts are "pinned down" and somewhat arbitrary. But the language of everyday life, including political-moral activity, is ordinary language. The concepts linked to ordinary language are not arbitrary but shared because they are transmitted in the culture, acquired, and revised rationally through historical-social reasoning. Norms of interpersonal relations and social conduct are, by definition, shared rules or standards, which also may be questioned or validated through rational argumentation concerning what is in the best interest of all concerned.

I cannot here deal with the consequences to the culture, society, and personality of closing off these forms of rationality in adopting the positivistic view of science. I will limit remarks to what it has done to home economists:

(a) It has made us conceptually naive and dogmatic in our acceptance of meanings. *Evidence:* We have never as a profession sought to comprehend and agree rationally on the meaning of concepts central to statements of mission over time: autonomous or free persons, democratic society, education. Further evidence: We uphold a pluralistic and privatistic view of meanings—my meaning is as good as your meaning—without advancing any reasons in an effort to validate our claim. Still further: We talk past one another in pseudo-communication assuming mutual understanding when there is none: we have difficulty understanding complex thought expressed in serious writing and speech for we lack both the concepts and the will to reason.

(b) It has made us morally naive and dogmatic regarding norms of rightness. *Evidence:* We do not recognize the moral implications of what we do—we never even talk about them although they are readily discernible to those educated to see such things. We leave values to monological selection by the individual expecting no rational and public justification of his claim. But his acting upon his values affects the lives of other people who have a right and an obligation to enter into the selection and validation of values. This monological selection of values we support on the grounds (a) that freedom of choice is desirable and (b) that empiracle science is value-neutral. But does freedom of choice occur when the individual is bound by his own ignorance and self-interest in choosing? Because empirical science is value-neutral, may not its use be for evil as well as good? Do we not have an uncontrolled technology that serves special interests?

Empirical science is fragmented into compartments. In adopting the positivistic view of knowledge, the subject matter of home economics has become fragmented. If we do indeed seek to serve the family in the interests of protecting and nurturing the individual and of contributing to a democratic society, we assume that life within the family and in the family's relation to society is a fragmented and compartmentalized one. That is an extremely naive conception.

Because we have continued to follow unreflectively the views that dominated the Lake Placid Conference on Home Economics and because these views encouraged naivete, a certain opportunism, and self-deception among us, we face a number of problems today as a profession and a discipline.

Disloyalty to our own aspirations. We have throughout our history had a number of aspirations—aspirations to which we are disloyal.

We aspire to helping the family because of its significance in the lives of individuals and in society. But we have helped to strip the family of its authority and have unwittingly taken a position against the family and the individual as we serve other powerful interests that disintegrate the family.

We aspire to keeping abreast of the times, of serving the family in light of contemporary social conditions. But we are naive about contemporary social realities—with the "wool pulled over our eyes," we look only at surface appearances without recognizing the contradictions and conflicts that exist and without probing what exists for implications to the individual, to the family, and to a democratic society.

We aspire to being a significant profession serving society in ways that are politically and morally worthy. But we do not distinguish between a service-oriented profession and a commercial business enterprise.

We aspire to having a discipline that provides the knowledge needed to fulfill the mission we claim to have. But there is undisciplined thought and action in the fragments of information dispensed, much of which is irrelevant to the mission we claim.

Internal discrepancies. There are discrepancies in beliefs within home economics and between what we say and what we do.

We look upon ourselves as an educated group. But we have not learned the norms and procedures available to us in traditions of the educated culture and by use of which a group develops its identity through communication. We adopt conceptual meanings and social norms haphazardly—and often from the mass culture—as if there were no established intellectual norms and procedures for validating them.

We claim to believe in free or autonomous persons. But we do not develop the intellectual and social capacities of individuals, including home economists, that enable them to be autonomous persons, nor do we take a stand against social practices that contstrain and hinder the development of those capacities. We encourage and we develop among ourselves both dependency and dogmatism.

We claim to believe in a democratic society. But we take an authoritarian position in seeking to promote and maintain certain totalitarian forces in society and in upholding a mode of professional action which is manipulative and repressive.

We claim, as a profession that requires systematic knowledge for enlightened action, to be rational. But there are numerous irrationalities among us: (a) We do not make a practice of and cannot rationally justify our claims to rightness of norms, to comprehensibility of concepts, and to sincerity of our intentions: (b) We are not a community that seeks mutuality of understanding and rational consensus among ourselves. (c) We deceive ourselves by putting forth certain norms as for the good of all when in reality those norms serve special interests, (d) We systematically conceal social contradictions and social conflict both in society at large and among ourselves.

Consequences of these disloyalties to our aspirations and internal discrepancies. As a consequence of the present intellectual and normative disarray in home economics, there exist conditions of unrest, disillusionment, and even feelings of futility among able home economists. There are still many dedicated and concerned home economists, but there are also many who use home economics for opportunistic self-interest. Once attracting some of the most scholastically able students as recruits to enter the profession, the situation has changed in recent years. Feistritzer Associates, a private organization that studies trends in education, reported that among 1,982 college-bound seniors planning to enter one of thirty-six possible fields of study, those planning to enter home economics ranked thirty-fourth in scholastic aptitude (9). Only those planning to enter ethnic studies or vocational education ranked lower. While scholastic aptitude is not a sufficient condition, it is a necessary condition to benefit adequately from college education to become a competent professional.

But there are consequences also beyond those internal to home economics. Our friendly critics in other professions and disciplines once saw home economics as promising potential and sought to help by offering constructive criticism. Now most have lost respect for us because of our naivete and failure to fulfil our promise. We have tended to look on such friendly criticism as failure to understand home economics when the truth is that our critics have often understood us better than we have understood ourselves.

Future of Home Economics

To paraphrase a suggestion by a U.S. president: "Ask not what the future promises home economics but what we in home economics must promise and deliver to the future."

We are victims of our own logic. But once understanding how this is so, we have already made the first step toward freeing ourselves from our self-imposed constraints. For this self-understanding, it would help to understand our history more adequately than these few minutes and this paper allow. Among reasoning people, such self-understanding becomes rational self-criticism, not to be confused with self-flagellation. We come to see how what we have done as a consequence of accepting ideological beliefs is contradictory to the ideals and hopes we have as a profession. We also see how these contradictions we have embraced have their source in historical-social conditions in home economics and in society at large. But the history of home economics after today remains to be made dependent upon what we choose and exert ourselves to make it.

If we are to fulfil the promise that some early home economists saw for their profession in the ideals and aspirations we still quote from our older literature, we must have the courage and the will and must gain the insight to change ourselves. I do not say that such change will be easy or that it will be without conflict and resistance. But I believe that there is a core of home economists who are already concerned, who do reason, who welcome filling in the gaps of cognitive development that their socialization into home economics has neglected, and who are willing to risk involvement of themselves with others in efforts as rational discourse. It is these people who must take the lead. There will be resistance from those with vested interests in turf-manship and power, from those too fixed and threatened to change themselves and from those unwilling to risk short-term losses for long-term gains. But part of the political struggle which must go on within home economics involves agreement (among those willing to undertake the struggle) on tactics for overcoming resistances. One thing is certain: we can not correct mistakes of the past by continuing to make them.

We need to develop and use the capacities of home economists for complex thought and for mutuality of relations. Only then will we develop faith and confidence in ourselves and remove habits of dogmatism and dependence. We need to do this not only in new generations of home economists but among those now in the profession. We can do this as we reexamine our mission, our discipline, and areas of service. This we must do as thinking and speaking persons, not as passive listeners. But the process must also be other than what some have called "a pooling of ignorance": we must make use of the resources of the educated culture, for example, theoretical analyses of concepts, of modes of rationality, of society.

I suggest that a good place to start is with a reinterpretation of the original mission of home economics. A profession does not change its mission whimsically but seeks to interpret it more adequately. This means that we need to comprehend and agree rationally on the concepts of free persons and a democratic society, on the relation of the two as well as on the place of the family in developing and protecting both. Only then can we understand our political-moral role as a profession.

Our discipline, as subject matter and modes of rationality, follows aim or mission as Marion Talbot sought to convince home economists eighty years ago and as Effie Raitt pointed out in the 1930s. It cannot be rationally developed as independent of that mission as ours was and still is. Here we need to differentiate conceptually among different forms of questions the subject matter is to address relative to the mission. We must become knowledgeable about different modes of rationality and use each to address the form of question for which it is logically appropriate. We must be more analytic of contemporary society calling upon levels and depths of analysis that go beyond *Reader's Digest* and best-sellers in the culture industry to scholarly work. We need to develop an attitude and competence to seek out the implications of existing social conditions and to ask whether other alternatives would be better for those we seek to serve.

We need to be able to engage properly in rational argumentation among ourselves: to expect and to provide rational grounds for what we believe and do, to validate the reasons given, to change our beliefs and our practices when we see that they are not adequately grounded. We can profit from critique that discloses our irrationalities. We need constantly to ask ourselves, "Whose interests do we really serve?"

In conclusion, I know that I have shocked you. But I can only hope that it has been a shock of enlightenment and motivation that will lead to freeing ourselves from our own internal constraints of naivete and irrationalities and from dependence on repressive external social forces. The time has come when we can no longer be blind and deaf to self-criticism. We cannot undo mistakes of the past, but we can correct them if we will. It will take courage and the very best thinking of which we are capable.

References

1. Mueller, H. J. *The Uses of the Past.* Oxford, Eng.: Oxford University Press, 1952.

2. Brown, M.M. *Philosophical Studies of Home Economics, vol. 1: Our Practical-Intellectual Heritage.* East Lansing: College of Human Ecology, Michigan State University (forthcoming).

3. Noble, D.F. *America by Design: Science, Technology, and the Rise of Corporate Capitalism.* New York: Alfred A. Knopf, 1977; Gilbert, J. *Designing the Industrial State.* New York: Quadrangle Books, 1972; Wirth, A.G. *Education and the Technological Society.* Scranton, Pa.: International Textbook, 1972.

4. *Proceedings of the Lake Placid Conference in Home Economics.* Tenth Annual Meeting (1908), 20.

5. *Proceedings of the Lake Placid Conference in Home Economics.* Sixth Annual Meeting (1904), 31.

6. Wiebe, R. H. *The Search for Order: 1877-1920.* New York: Hill and Wang, 1967.

7. *Proceedings of the Lake Placid Conference in Home Economics.* Fourth Annual Meeting (1902), 56.

8. Hunt, C.L. *The Life of Ellen H. Richards.* Washington, D.C.: American Home Economics Association (1958), 183, see also pp. 151 and 165.

9. "Testing Reveals Teacher 'Crisis'" *The Oregonian (17 March 1983), A 10.*

TABLE 1

Conflicting Views at the Lake Placid Conference

Richards, Dewey, Norton	Cboum, Talbot, Andrews
View of human beings	
Capable of being made into "efficient workers" and "efficient citizens" of the state; emphasis on what men did in complying with externally defined standards in the existing society. The individual is plastic stuff which society molds—an object to be manipulated. The inner life of the individual is simple: one of seeking his own self-interest.	Active users of language and thought. Capable of complex intellectual activity and of moral action of capacities; are developed through reason; emphasis on "the powers latent within"—on "moral and intellectual freedom" through "a mind restored to consciousness by his own sovereign faculty" of reason. The individual is formed through interaction with his sociocultural world.
View of the home	
A symbol of the financial and moral status of those who live there—who spend and manage efficiently. A place where work by the woman was to be done in a way that made it a "perfected machine," concerned with efficient results as in business and industry. The family is not as capable of teaching the young the "rules of right living" as organized agencies of society.	The center of mutuality and rational consciousness concerned with promoting the moral and intellectual capacities of its members. But "the obligations of home life are not by any means limited to its own four walls"; they extend also to the problems of the larger society which hinder the family in fulfilling its obligations. Further, "men and women are alike concerned in understanding the processes, activities, obligations and opportunities which make the home and family effective parts of the social fabric."
View of society	
Vertical view of climbing from one social class to a higher one through the "management of things" and social engineering. Social evolution is a natural process of improvement and progress. Since all social change represents progress, the individual and the family improve by conforming to the existing society and its "progress." In "modernization." However, society is static since it can be studied "en masse" and knowing the causes of social behavior, such behavior can be predicted and controlled.	Society is to provide "the fullest opportunity" for "not any favored class" but for all individuals. Human life is social (interpersonal) life in which mutual understanding and agreement are necessary. Society is a human construction which is changed politically–morally through increased understanding of historically specific sources of domination—through developing individual capacities and cooperative political struggle. While there should be conformity to those social regulations mutually agreed upon as in the interest of all the people, there should not be conformity to forces of domination and repression often embodied in social structures and processes.

Meaning of rationality

Rational knowledge is derived only from the methods of the empirical sciences. Rational action consists of the following of technical (how-to-do-it) rules derived from the findings of empirical science. Even political-moral activity was to be the application of empirical science to "eradicate evil."	Rational knowledge comes from a "multiplicity of ways, study, analysis"; no one mode of rationality is adequate, eg., technical-empirical. There are also forms of rationality in the acquisition and use of language, in communication which develops a "unity of thought and sentiment" and which binds people "into a common life and inspires a common loyalty." Such communication carried with it a "mental and moral discipline." Rationality involves a consciousness in which reasons are advanced and argued.

Ends to be served through education in home economics

Scientific management of work of the home for efficiency and economy using the principles of management in business and industry. If the physical and economic aspects of the home are improved, moral, intellectual, and aesthetic aspects of home life will progress.	Development of individual capacities (freedom) within the family; emancipation from conditions of domination and repression in society. Through raising consciousness of the implications of "conditions of the physical, social, moral, aesthetic and spiritual conditions of the home to the individual and to society at large," not only will individual capacities be developed but "the conditions of society" can be changed to provide a more just and democratic society.

View of knowledge in home economics

Generated from observation for the power to control things and people: empirical sciences and technical rules (as how-to rules of "right living"). Knowledge is monological in that it is used by one person to control his environment.	Generated from reflective reason, interpersonal communication and rational agreement, and observation. While knowledge from observation in the empirical sciences can be used monologically to control nature, social interaction and social reason are required for understanding and validating the concepts, norms, and rules of the sociocultural world.

View of organization of the discipline

Fragmented parcels each organized around performance of some household task. One-dimensional: how to produce certain ends in controlling the environment.	Complex integration of knowledge from philosophy, history, literature, and the empirical sciences organized for understanding the relations among individual development, conditions in the home and family, and social realities. Multi-dimensional: concerned with moral and intellectual freedom as well as physical and economic well-being through the "common life" of the family, the educated culture, and the society.

187